WITHDRAWN

Mother Spring

A Three Continents Book

Mother Spring

Driss Chraibi

*Translated from the French
by Hugh Harter*

LYNNE
RIENNER
PUBLISHERS

BOULDER
LONDON

Published in the United States of America by
Lynne Rienner Publishers, Inc.
1800 30th Street, Boulder, Colorado 80301
www.rienner.com

First published in French by Editions du Seuil. © 1982 Editions du Seuil

ISBN 978-0-89410-401-5 (hc. : alk. paper)
ISBN 978-0-89410-402-2 (pbk. : alk. paper)

Printed and bound in the United States of America

 The paper used in this publication meets the requirements
of the American National Standard for Permanence of
Paper for Printed Library Materials Z39.48-1992.

Once again Islam will become the stranger it was in the beginning.

—The Prophet Mohammed

This book is dedicated to *Oum-er-Bia* [Mother Spring], the Moroccan river at whose mouth I was born. I also dedicate it to the Sons of the Earth, the Berbers, who are its heroes; to the Islam of the early times: the exile that saw it born from nudity and the desert, just like the Islam of the apogee: Cordoba; to the Indians of America penned up in reserves and who at present are interrogated like so many salutary doubts in the certitudes of civilization; to the Palestinians, the Celts, the Occitans, the so-called primitive tribes; to all the minorities who, when all's said and done, are the great majority of our world and whose brother I am.

D.C.

Table of Contents

Notice

This is not a history book, but a novel. If it has its source in history, the galloping imagination of the author, who resembles me like a brother, is very much a part of it. Consequently, any resemblence of any sort to historical events can only be pure coincidence, a felicitous encounter. Furthermore, what has neither changed nor aged since the beginning of time is the earth. And I have always had a madness for light and for water. If these two elements should ever cease to be, the history of man would run dry . . . .

EPILOGUE

THE PRESENT

Raho Aït Yafelman was walking along the roadway one pure August morning in the year of Christian grace nineteen hundred eighty-two—a very tall and very thin Berber whose face bore the stamp of peace. What year could it be among the Arabs, according to the Hegira? No doubt they did not know themselves. Up to now, they counted dates and money in the manner of the *Zeropeans*. Like the Arabs, Raho was a Muslim at heart, if not in thinking. He had learned their language, or at least their common vocabulary (and a few words of French) so that he could go through his human existence without too much poverty, racket, or misunderstanding. Far distant in the obscurity of time, Destiny had sounded the voice of arms, and now, centuries and centuries later, the sons of the soil, the Imazighen, had somehow to go on surviving in their own country. What had to be done had to be done: to accept fate. But one had to avoid what one could avoid: dying.

The history of the Arab conquest had come down to him orally, in bits and pieces. In the course of generations, it had been somewhat watered down, transformed into a collection of fairy tales which had the power to make the Elders of the village shake their heads and put small children to sleep. But, by Allah and the Prophet, Raho had never found out if these immigrants and their descendants were five centuries behind or ahead of the Nazareens, those other people who left their territories one day, perhaps never to return. In act and word, were they so different from one another when you summed it all up?

By turns, making war then negotiating, the Arabs had imposed their order, but time was time, Man's sovereign. And words were only words, however one moved one's tongue about one's mouth; in two or three millenia, they would end up being wiped away from all memory. Every bit. The mountains, the deserts, and the plains, whose crust the civilizations of speech had only scratched, would remain. It was a question of patience, that's all. From now until then, at least as long as there was still some water, Raho Ait Yafelman would go on calming the thirst of the thirsty, brothers and strangers.

3

As every morning, he awoke at dawn, high up on the bare hill in the village of Tselfat. There was, of course, a cock, but it was so old and sickly that it could hardly hear its own voice. It passed half of its life sleeping in front of Raho's door and the other half wandering between the thorn bushes and cob-walled houses, trying to survive. Chickens frightened it but not the humans, who chased it away from their dwellings with loud cries, as if it had the plague; they were incomprehensible and belligerent, but sometimes they threw some scraps of food which it located as quickly as they hit the ground and for which the female fellow creatures disputed bitterly. The cock's hunger was insistent—and insistent the memory of the worms of its youth, fat and succulent. By what marvel could they have grown in this arid earth, cooked and recooked by the sun? Even it could hardly stand on its two feet while searching for shade and forgetfulness.

Day after day, Raho suffered at the very sight of this miserable fowl that resembled him like a brother. Fatalistic and destitute, he turned his eyes away as he did his ablutions thinking of God rather than of His creatures. So Islam was only the religion of the resigned, the oppressed, and other rejects? Certainly not! Most certainly not! There were Muslims who fared very well, potbellied and powerful, who were happy as well. How did they manage to lack nothing, either on earth or in heaven? They even had airplanes, to be closer to the Lord. What was their formula?

"It's simple," Raho said to himself, "very simple. There were two Islams, one of the privileged and the other . . . the other for the greatest number of the children of Eve and Adam who have never had anything through the centuries and never will have anything in the centuries to come except faith and hope."

His face devoid of expression, he quickly recited the Koranic verse of contrition:

"I take refuge by thy side, Lord!"

He took up a handful of sand and poured it over his short-cropped head because he knew he had blasphemed, so great had been the temptation to blaspheme. He was angry with himself, and that was why he spit between his feet, to root out the Middle Ages that survived in him despite generations of Islam. He was not at all a Muslim worthy of the name, that's the truth of it! He still had to master his pagan forces, to wait patiently still and forever. What significance did time have in the face of eternity? Or daily reality compared to the paradise promised by the Koran in the Beyond?

This cock, whose false notes would have wished themselves a chant of triumph, probably did not know that the shade was more hardy than the prey. It had no religion of any kind, and yet, it was so old! And no kind of age could go backwards toward the first ardent youth when everything was to be begun, everything to be hoped for, everything to be loved. The "Book that returned souls" affirmed, however, in terms as clear as the light in August:

All sterile and dead earth, we shall transform into fertile green.

And wherever they may be scattered, we shall gather up your
bones, whosoever you may be. We shall bring you to life again.

"Amen!" said Raho. "He is right." He had tears in his eyes as he did
every time he recited a versicle, even mentally. And he spoke in a low
voice from fear that the atheist cock would hear him. He carefully avoided
looking at that half-plucked animal with the bald head and the white
eyes. "He told the truth, Lord!" he repeated with a sort of tranquil despair.
"If he says that death does not exist, well, it doesn't exist. Neither does
misery, nor illness nor the solitude of the elderly, nothing that causes
suffering to man or beast in this world. Just think, it suffices to shut one's
eyes and to have faith in Him. He knows, He does."

He crouched down on his heels and looked at the earth for a long
while. No, not the earth of the others with its benedictions of green, where
even the superfluous flourished, nor other lands lower down or far away
in God's or the Devil's other countries, with gushing springs, melodious
streams and, above them, clouds bursting with joyous rain—but this one,
his earth where he lived with his tribe. Was it true, as the "legend" went in
Derb Sahrawa, the section where beggarly dreamers lived, that with a bit
of manure from *Lamirika* and a few modern prayers, as it rained in such
abundance on the other side of the horizon in the desert of the Arabs
covered with oil wells, this clinking gravel pit that was white hot as soon as
it dawned would become once more what it had been at the beginning: a
hill planted with trees and an equal number of lives?

"Praise be to *Lamirika*" he prayed fervently. "Praise be to its faithless
sons, however they may be! Yes, indeed."

He washed his face . . . his hands and feet. Three times, according to
ritual. He had confidence in all things and in every being—perhaps even in
himself. What the genius of men had destroyed to the very roots, the genius of
other men might well bring to life again, who knows? He did not empty
the pail of water in which he had just done his ablutions. It would serve
him again the next day. Water was water. He thought about the Oum-er-
Bia, Mother Spring, the nutritious river at whose mouth his ancestors had
lived...

That's how it was every morning: a man from the mountain awoke on
the mountain, as peaceful as the mountain itself. The doubts and fears of
the night before had all been washed away in the black waters of the
night. He opened his eyes and the door of his little shack, and just as
quickly, there sparkled in him all the springtimes of the world, because
there in front of him on the far horizon, was a new dawn that would light
everything up. And at the same time, almost at the very second, every
distress in the world fell on his shoulders as he saw the blind cock, whose
song had once sounded a call of life to life and who was there now, a
witness, wandering about half-starved in eternal nights without understanding anything or anyone. What could he, Raho, the son of the naked
earth, do to help it? Should he twist its neck?

One did not finish off the infirm, even in the name of what we call pity.

When a man like himself had passed all of his existence between heaven and earth, he could only accept life, as fully in its adversities as in its benefits. He knew very well that the only response to a prayer was its own echo, and that holding his hands out palm up toward that cloudless, celestial vault would not fill them with rain. That is why, every morning, he would say:

"Tomorrow, may Allah will it!"

His face rigid and distracted, he repeated in a trembling voice:

"Tomorrow, *incha Allah*, the cock will be cured of his ills, or I will find him dead at last, peaceful and at peace."

One after the other, he placed his hands flat against the earth, with his fingers spread out . . . . Then, with his mouth open and his eyes closed, he drank in the morning air until he thought his lungs would burst. He exhaled. Slowly he pronounced the magic formula that succeeded so well for him:

"Raho, empty your head!"

His spirit was freed instantaneously, cleared as if by will of the bones and debris of the twentieth century, Raho Ait Yafelman turned in the direction of Mecca (toward the east, the daily renewal, the sun, master of worlds) and prostrated himself . . . . He said his first monotheistic prayer of the day, the prayer of dawn. Joyfully he recited the living words that men, in the name of life, had captured in a book of paper and ink that one read with one's eyes:

> *Wa shamsi wa douhaha! . . . . By the sun and its brilliance! And*
> *by the night when it descends, and by the moon when it rises!*
> *By the heavens and He who raised it! . . . . And by the human*
> *soul and He who gave it stability! . . . .*

By the human soul and He who gave it stability . . . That was eternal, beyond all of the senses that communicated with the brain, well before thought. As he peacefully recited his prayer, his soul far from any turbulence, it was as if the first men from the earliest times who had nothing, possessed nothing, and fled from Mecca to found the human community in the Arab desert, had spoken with him that morning on that arid hill of Tselfat. And if only the rocks and the sand of this desert were to survive for thousands of years, this sand and these rocks would still preserve the traces of the gigantic emotion of other times when what is now called religion was the love of one's neighbor, of the weak and the poor, of the orphan—of the stranger. Raho had lived that thirteen centuries earlier. He was sure of it. And the History of man, in its developments ever since, had been nothing more than a series of nothings full of wind. Raho knew that also with absolute certainty. He rose up.

With disjointed movements, Raho sat on his rump, opened his eyes, and greeted humanity to his right and his left, saying:

"Peace be with you! Peace!"

He saw the cock lying on its side near a little pile of charcoal with its wings stretched out behind, stiff for all time. He said:

"May God welcome you in paradise and in his mercy!"

All sorrow was both infinite and ephemeral, as was all joy. But was this not true of all human undertakings to find the only real happiness, that one could hardly ever attain: peace with one's self and with one's fellow man. As he contemplated the corpse of the rooster who had so proudly impregnated a multitude of hens, he saw the familiar fig tree in the little stony clearing. It was the only tree in the village, but it was heavy with ripe fruit, most of them bursting. It belonged to everyone, to the thirty-four families of the tribe, as did the goat, the mule, and the red donkey. With the blessing of the beneficent earth, there would probably be a second harvest in the fall, with as many figs as Hajja and the other women (all related in varying degrees) could dry in the sun on flat stones before stringing them together in rosaries with palm fiber, to take later on down to the town, to the *souk* of Sidi Kacem Bou Asriya.

Some years there was nothing more than leaves on the fig tree—who knew why! Nevertheless, whether it was as dry as a dried-up old maid or as full of progeny as Mamma of Africa, it provided shade in the summertime, a semblance of coolness. On Friday, the assembly of the two councils, one of the Elders and the other of the active members of the village, met at its feet. Oh those interminable words where every point of view was taken into account, listened to religiously, developed from its source through its minute meanderings, you might say from the beginnings of the world! Other versions, just as detailed, would be woven in as well, concerning the same facts or the same dispute, rolling in like successive waves that covered and renewed one another, with effusions of laughter by way of commentary. As the flow of words was very slow and time passed in the long and empty silences used for serious reflection, the meetings often went on till dawn. One did what had to be done, but the decision was made, or approximately so, by a majority of voices. And when no democratic forum emerged, well, they put off until the following Friday the "devil's tail" (the thorny case). Time would give birth to plenty of new weeks, fall would follow summer, and then winter; who could know if from that time to this, with a bit of aging and a grain of philosophy, the "mule heads" would not change their minds? And then, arguing was always a pleasure.

Of course, yes, of course! There was always the State. Even if one wanted to avoid recognizing it at all cost, you knew it very well. The State took it upon itself to remind you of its orders by force. One could say to it: "Monsieur Leta, fly off on your farts and let us blunder on. You always up there on top, and us always down below, that's life!"

There was the State's representative, coming down from on high or up from below, surrounding the village on all sides—and why? He was given different names depending on his hierarchical degrees: *Sidna* (R'Masta), *Son of Adam* (gifted bureaucrats with a certain gentleness and enormous patience), That-Thing-That-You-Know or else The-House-of-Hidden-Things (the government), The Son of Calamity (the tax collector), the

Sons of the Wind (judges, lawyers, magistrates), the So-and-So's (personalities, celebrities, footballers, crooners, and . . . the Americans), the National Police or the Sellers (the cops), the Grasshoppers (soldiers and gendarmes), etc. So many strangers who did not even take the trouble to sit down under the fig tree and chat civilly for some five or six hours. Certain representatives, like R'Masta, had never come to the village, the Lord only knows why.

Those from the plain and the cities who climbed up panting did not know the good manners that transformed the couch grass into ears of wheat and the stranger into a brother. Not even a gift for the Elders nor a dried date for Hajja! And, after all, she was the mother of the tribe. Nothing but the threatening Law that the State's representatives brought with them like a bludgeon, with a mixture of officialdom and terror. Did they perhaps expect to be beaten up?

As they lived with the rhythm of the seasons, the people of Tselfat got along willy-nilly with Monsieur Leta. They were made to declare their surnames, first names and nicknames, the place and the presumed date of their birth. And their forebears, born where? What do you mean "over that way?" What village, what area? All right, all right, so they're deceased, God rest their souls. But when were they born more or less? You don't remember? . . . And you have children? Boys, girls? How many of each? What does that mean, "half-and-half?" For each case, two witnesses were necessary . . . No, no, not the whole village. Get away, get away from me! I said: "Only *two* witnesses."

Empty, senseless questions, sterile harassments without a name, that went on for almost five years, with police and scribblers, for nothing more than taking a census of the some two hundred villagers who came and went, either nomadic or sedentary, however they wished (perhaps one hundred eighty-two? Let's call it two hundred ten!), all relatives, all united on one front, brothers since the time of King Jugurtha.

Several, with their Berber memory, had never had either patronymic or first name—and why should they since you come into the world without a stitch on? ("Were you born with eyeglasses, So-and-So?") they were simply called the "old one," "the wise one," "the limper," and that was all. Or else the "charcoal burner"; that woman you see over there, as she is the one who makes charcoal and goes to sell it in the Sidi Kacem Bou Asriya, but next season, Allah willing, she will be the "cheese maker." It's her turn, you understand? No? And this woman is the "Teller of tales by the light of the moon." Why, everybody knows her! The mother of the tribe had once made the pilgrimage to Mecca on foot. That's why she has the right to the title of "Haaja." And even she had forgotten her first name, really forgotten it. Oh you can insist, So-and-So, she can't remember any more! Of course she's not making fun of you. What good is it anyway to want to know everything? It's a waste of time . . .

Now, the State attached a great deal of basic importance to the control of names. It wanted impartial facts and figures.

"Write down whatever you want, all you So-and-So's. We agree."

Worn out by the struggle, they were given family identification booklets, interchangeable, with which they had no idea of what to do: they were totally illiterate. Bourguine thought of converting them into cash, as he knew some "no-name-no-homer's" and perhaps he could barter for some.

Hajja said: "No."

She declared these papers worthless; they were not adorned with any pictures, like paper money or the legends of King Solomon.

The villagers lifted their feet, dragged them through the dust, and met under the tree to have a consultation. The mint tea was boiling hot, the sun was torrid, and the discussion was heated until evening. Haaja's point of view was adopted easily and unanimously. The documents were placed in her charge. To be more exact, each head of family placed his identification booklet at Haaja's feet, as though it were a dead rat held by two fingers by the tail. Only she could purify these scribblings of civilization, since she had once been in the sacred places of Islam.

Haaja said: "*Bismillah!* In the name of the Most High!"

And she made a little pile of these "things," flattened them out with the palm of her hand until they were like a paper brick, that she placed in a bucket and lowered into one of the village wells, almost down to water level, twenty to twenty-five meter's under the earth's surface.

She said: "This way no one will see them, unless they have the eyes of a dragon. And we are human beings, the rest of us. If the sons of the plains ever come back here, well, they'll find their 'things' still in fresh condition."

When the reign of identity cards began, the booklets were needed to prepare them. Haaja pulled on her rope, hoisted up the bucket and its content to the light of day, and as everyone watched, said:

"There. There you have your sacred deposit."

Curiously enough, the booklets had not been mildewed. Perhaps they had great durability! But which one belonged to whom? No one could find out, certainly not the bureaucrats who came from the city. They weren't the same ones who came before, but they resembled them in language and in their lack of comprehension of even the simplest things of life. One of them wore glasses, and all of them were literate, wise men. Then why were they ranting and raving? Why did their eyes become opaque and turn as red as the sauce of a *tajine* with its pepper, chickpeas, and lamb's feet? It was their property. They had confided it to the people of the village who were returning it intact. What was the problem?

"Which one in there is Aït Yafelman?" shouted the bureaucrat of the state who suddenly was transformed into an officer in a state of siege. (He shuffled the booklets like a pack of cards.)

"That's me," answered Raho Aït Yafelman, with great courtesy.

"That's me," added several unidentified persons, including some impudent kids.

The city man turned his bulk toward the body of Aït Yafelman and shouted rudely:

"You over there, what are you called?"

"Huh?"

"What's your name?"

"Yafelman."

"Your first name? The FIRST name?"

"Mohand"

"And you?"

"Mohand"

"You too?"

"The same. Mohand, like my brother. Mohand the Elder."

"And you?"

"Moh."

"Oh, come on!"

"Yes, my name is Mohand, but they call me Moh to distinguish me from the little one over there. He's called Moh Mohand. It's that simple."

"And you, madame? Answer me! What's your name?"

"The baker woman."

"What?"

"I bake the bread, but it isn't ready yet. If you'll wait a bit, I'll give you a nice round one. It won't be long, just about an hour."

"Family! What's your family name? You're not going to tell me that you're called Moh or Mohand Aït Yafelman? *You too*? Word of honor, I won't believe it. Mohand is a man's name, and right away I saw that you are a woman."

"Ah no, monsieur. I don't let my tongue get carried away. God knows that I don't know how to lie. My family is the Boukhrissi."

"So, finally," exclaimed the man with the glasses as he wiped the perspiration from his forehead, neck, and ears. (It was the good sweat of satisfaction.) Finally! We're starting to see things clearly!"

"Oh yes, monsieur," approved the baker woman. "It's clear, as you say. I am a Boukhrissi and my husband over there is an Aït Yafelman, called Si Mo Mohand Aït Yafelman, the brother of Raho, and I'm like him. An Aït Yafelman. It's simple, but if you want to write down Boukhrissi, that's fine. The little boy who answered you a little while ago is just called Moh, nothing more. He's my son. By the grace of God, I may have a daughter this spring. Right, my man."

The man in question did not stand out from the compact group in any way. As he laughed easily at the mention of the coming birth and the festivities that would follow it, everyone laughed too. The sky was clear. Haaja began to speak and gave a luminous explanation of the family situation. She took the hand of the bureaucrat in her own and said:

"He has a silly laugh, but you must not see any malice in it, my son. He's my nephew. He is proud of what you know. His wife isn't like him.

She lowers her eyes when she talks about what you do with your wife, if you're married. If God gives them a daughter in the springtime, she will be a Boukhrissi, as is the custom. And, if it's a boy, it will be an Aït Yafelman. You understand, the wife of Si Moh Mohand is the niece of the aunt of my late brother, may God protect his soul! And her husband is the second cousin of my husband. I know all of them as I'm their grandmother. They're all my children. So . . . ."

She was talking in the afternoon. And night fell.

The next morning, a moustache had replaced the intellectual eye-glasses. A black moustache to make an impression. The man was equipped with a loudspeaker.

He said: "There are four cardinal points, no more, no less. The north, the south, the east, the west. Understand?"

The villagers looked at one another, flabbergasted. This son of the twentieth century did not know the two fundamental points of man: the earth underneath his feet and the sky over his head. The earth, however, was as hard as Hindu steel, and the sun already like lead, at nine o'clock in the morning. There were pounding boots, helmets, black glasses—beings from another age or from another planet, all over the place. Four signposts, set into bases of heavy stones, cut the air of the village into a sort of square. It had been impossible to dig the smallest hole in the stony ground. A pneumatic drill had been necessary.

The people of the village were not unhappy with all this excitement, even if it came with the roaring of combustion engines. After all, in what century had the last camel caravan come through? The man with the black moustache sounded his loudspeaker like a drum out of hell:

"Attention! Attention! Now hear this, all of you! This is what you are going to do. The women will go toward the post set to the west. The children will go to the east, there where the sun is shining now. You understand, kids? You'll go in the opposite direction from the post. When I give the order, the men will go to the north. The confusion will be resolved after that because the heads of family will be left, and they will go to that south post. Clear enough, right?"

Wrong. However startling this reasoning may have seemed to them, neither adults nor children gave any sign of it. Huddled together in one compact group, they contented themselves with patiently waiting to be shown how one could cut a son of Adam of male sex who was at one and the same time a head of family in two equal pieces. They didn't say a word, didn't make a move. Alone near the thornbush, the red donkey shook its pointed ears. One ear lay flat full length pointed in the direction of the government man (I think it was the left one); the other stood straight up toward the sky, like a living minaret.

"Attention! Attention! Women to the west! Let's go!"

The women lifted their feet, raised their small children onto their shoulders, and braced them around their arms at the end of which they dragged some other little ones. Then they got under way. Next came the men of the tribe who were an integral part of their spouses, mothers, sisters, and relatives in varying degrees.

But nothing could make the exercise in futility work, neither threats nor police control, not even philosophical discussions that lasted as long as the sun kept on shining. They had been one single tribe since the beginning of the world's creation and they would remain so until the end of time. They could not be separated, even on the rolls of government, even deceptively with words. When reason rests on a foundation of sand, it crumbles into anger. And if Allah the All-Powerful had ordained a human race, then they had always been a community, long before His word resounded in the Koran.

Everyone, male and female, said with a single voice: *Aha!* That meant a clear and resounding "yes." Yes, they understood the orders of R'Masta and the government. It was for their own good. Certainly. *Aha!* Yes! They shook their heads in affirmation that the officials words had penetrated their Berber skulls. And they shook their heads like a pendulum, force-fully, and said with the same courteous tone: *Oho!* No! No, nothing at all, they did not comprehend those orders or the good that would come from them. *Oho!* No! Absolutely not! If it's a benefit as you say, So-and-So, keep it for yourself. They had everything they needed; they were happy as they were, without identity cards or papers. It's very simple, you see, Monsieur.

They went right to the core of words, to the pit or the seeds. Certain words were empty of all sense, and once they were all worn out, the villagers carried on their dialogue in silence. To be more exact, they assembled under the fig tree, which hadn't budged an inch either, and looked at one another like sets of China dolls. The eyes of the Sons of the Earth were strangely limpid,.without a single blink. The sun was roasting hot from one horizon to the other, sky, earth, and everything in between. And then, the sun went down.

In their time, the Zeropeans had resolved the problem of the Aït Yafelman by not touching them. For their part, the *Imazighen* thought no better of their white guests' settlement. As a consequence, both commu-nities had lived side by side for some decades, those who were in the fertile plains and fields and those who inhabited the mountains that became more and more arid.

Neither war nor peace had resolved the differences in their points of view on existence. However rich and powerful they were, the Zeropeans, the sons of the Occident, were ignorant of the paths that lead man toward himself. Even so, they were knowledgeable about the smallest details of life. Raho's sister-in-law, "She Who Tells Tales by the Light of the Moon," asserted that they had put out the sun in their native land and replaced it with little artificial stars that hung from the ceilings of their houses. She said too that they hardly spoke to one another the way you and I do whole afternoons, neighbor to neighbor drinking mint tea, and that for words they had to use a kind of wire that they called *tillphoune*— without even seeing each other!

The confrontation took a different turn with the new masters. History had made an aboutface; they were once again among compatriots, as before. Religion had woven its sacred ties, and it could serve for some time to come. After all, the Arabs knew the value of patience. Weren't their ancestors born in a naked desert? And now a benediction of dollars rained down on that very desert! With a little diplomacy and a courageously democratic politic, this rebellious isle would be won over to the national community of the twentieth century.

And so it came about that one Friday in springtime (the fig tree was budding), a mayor was elected. By every single hand. They were all raised to the sky as a witness. An Aït Yafelman who had dressed in a white *gandoura* for the occasion . . . . Unless it was a Boukhrissi who owned the *gandoura*? Or a Basfao, who might have sold it the night before to a Boukhrissi and who wore it while he waited for payment next season? Who knows? And the aides to the new mayor were named Basfao, Boukhrissi, Aït Yafelman—or the other way around. It was quite simple.

Everybody was quite happy with himself and the state of affairs. The representatives of the governments had gone back to the capital, weighed down with thick packets of paper. The officials felt that their mission succeeded, and the Law had finally triumphed: by making an official of one of these bumpkins, by giving him responsibility, the tribe could be broken apart. Who, after all, had ever turned down an offer of power?

The new mayor called together the council the very next morning. If there was nothing worthy of being called a city hall in the village, there was the square which could hold some twenty persons easily. The deliberations were brief.

"Do you want to bother with all of this?"

"No."

"But can we pretend to carry on with it to avoid problems with those bores?"

"Yes."

"So it's voted."

At this point the mayor closed his hand in a fist and struck it against the palm of his left hand in a kind of official stamp. He took off his *gandoura* and became a plain member of the tribe again and said:

"Bourgine! Hitch up the mule and go tell them that the order of the day was voted without difficulty."

"Yes, uncle." Bourgine made a sort of whinnying sound. It was his way of laughing. "I'll go right away. The mule needs some exercise."

"Good," concluded the mayor. "And now that the government is satisfied, we're going to examine this same order of the day in Berber, according to custom, as we always have done."

The council of Elders and the active members of the village went over to sit under the fig tree and deliberated under the open sky until nightfall. And so it was with all the worries of the government, of whatever degree of importance, national, provincial, county or township: the mayor (it was never the same man; a member of the tribe put on the *gandoura*, another wore it the week after) had the vote taken unanimously, eyes closed, as fast as possible, explaining:

"There is a . . . or rather a . . . I don't know what the problem is, after all. What will they invent next? Shall we please them? Everybody agree? Good, it's voted. Bourgine, hitch up the mule."

Then came the real deliberations: not to bend even slightly the official *khakha* to the ancestral life of the tribe, but to protect it as if from the Devil, to hide it from the inspectors who swooped down on the village at untimely moments. The hiding-places were so cleverly placed in unknown spots, like some special mathematics, entangled in such labyrinths that not even an expert up from the city with all his rationality could have an inkling of their whereabouts. Of course, he asked for explanations, about local taxes for example. At that point, language immediately lost its logic if not its coherence in a torrent of details without apparent connections or consistency; incantatory language beatified any and all algebraic equations. Across from the interrogator sat an Elder of long experience and great serenity or a woman who knew the secrets of life as children had come out of her belly who, in their turn, had procreated.

He said quietly: "It is very simple, my son. You will understand in a little while. Wait patiently in your soul, and everything will become intelligible. The tax collection has been made, yes. You want some cumin? It bores into the innards and makes spaces for the dish that is next to come, and the mayor has done his duty as he should. There is no one more just than he in the whole countryside; everybody was happy to pay his dues as the law states, even the people who don't own so much as a rusty nail, from the first to the last of us. Take a lick of this hot pepper, it's delicious with giblets. So everything is in order, toss over your left shoulder all your worries; the sum you came to get is put safely away. Put this cushion behind your back, this house is yours.

"Bourgine, bring the couscous! Yes; you can. You still have a little empty spot and consequently you'll have a problem putting all the tax money in your automobile. Next month, God willing.

"Drink as much as you like, it's cool whey; it's *leben* like your mother made. Your memories are full of emotions, no doubt about it. Don't talk all the time, let me explain. We have always made it with goat's milk. You let it curdle in an earthenware jar in the ground, two to four days depending on the weather, then you decant it in a goatskin that you hang by two ends from the fork of a tree. But that's the way it's done. That's what you saw over there hanging from a branch of the fig tree. I'm coming, I'm coming. Everything in its time. Then you give the goatskin a push when you walk by, everybody adds his bit, above all the kids who have no patience with time; you swing it back and forth day after day until your ear hears a sort of lapping sound, like the voice of a little stream that rolls the pebbles in its bed.

"Yes! The money is there. Clear your head. That means that the butter is separated from the curds that are liquid again. All you have to do then is pass it through a sieve and transfer it to a wooden bucket. Drink some more! Isn't it cool? I shouldn't tell you this since you're our guest, but the municipal council had decided that this *leben* would be used to make some soft white cheeses whose sale would have plugged a little hole in the budget. Oh, a little hole that doesn't amount to anything. Count in with that the butter that separated from the whey that would have brought in more money, but what do you use but butter to grease the couscous, if not butter, precisely?

"There's nothing for you to worry about. You have the mind to explain to the government that we couldn't properly receive you without having some sort of celebration for you, and so we've deducted the future value of the butter from the sum. The government will understand. Tell them also that we have dipped into the reserve for the money to buy the couscous, lamb of highest quality, the vegetables, and the spices. Hospitality is sacred, that's for sure!"

There came more explanations in which imagination overflowed those sure frontiers recognized by the concert of nations and from which came . . . what? What do you want to say my brother? Of course, of course, the taxes have been collected, with such ease that not a piece of money was put into circulation. Yes that's right. Collected orally, as you guessed. It's the intention that counts, one's given word. Each one of us has made a promise, and you can be sure the tribe has always put honor higher than anything in the world. Consequently the mayor now has his city hall, his own house which he graciously puts at the disposal of the municipal council. And his family: his aged mother, his little ones of whom two are still tiny, his poor wife all have to live in the home of a neighbor who charges them room and board. Naturally, he doesn't have a single cent, like the rest of us. The mayor has sacrificed his private life so the law can be observed. He is doing some legal bartering: he lends his house, the brother takes in his family, and the expenditures balance out the receipts, more or less.

Certain obstinate bureaucrats (whose work it was to oversee the actions of their colleagues) were neither hungry nor thirsty. They knew nothing about hospitality. They didn't bother to sit down. They opened up their attache cases and their ledgers, and stood waiting, their eyes straight ahead. The people of the village were suddenly transformed into stone-age primitives who were incapable of surmounting the chain of mountains that separated the two languages.

An official interpreter was named. The Berber language became, all of a sudden, a totally private idiom that only the people of Tselfat used—something like: *Abbedegga? Aboudigou? Dibougou boudidada khnennek amzght heugh! Khoukhoublàà!* . . . and other "guttural sounds." They didn't understand a single thing, inventing as they went along a dialogue of the deaf. Other tribes that had come from miles around camped on the heights. Where they came from, no one knew; nor by what magic telephone, encircling the village, and ready to come to the help of the Aït Yafelman: they were the repository of the soul of an ancient people, and this soul had triumphed over all civilizations, in spite of the assaults of history. For the defenders of order, what could be done except to establish bonds that would be piled up on the papers already gathered? It was hot in this infernal countryside, above all in their hearts, and the least mistake would have provoked a conflagration from one tribe to another.

"Tomorrow," they said, as they packed up their baggage. "Next month, if God wills . . . . It will all be settled in a year, day by day, name of God! . . . ."

One year later, there was the joyous inauguration of the POS (Plan for the Occupation of the Soil), probably for the recuperation of the whole affair from the base up. Geometers and the specialists of the cadastral survey calculated every centimeter of the habitable surfaces. But tangents, sines, and cosines could not determine this age-old and anti-algebraic unknown factor: what belonged to whom? The Bafao, the Aït Yafelman, Boukhrissi, and other *chleuhs* swam in their logic like fish in the water, because what seemed a little bit hard to understand at first glance was simplicity itself, and that's what they explained to these users of tachometers and theodolites. They tried, at least:

"This house, you say? *This one here?* Whose is it? Wull, b'longs ta him, of course. Except for the wall at the end that belongs to the neighbor and, let's see, the third or the fourth of the court area that belongs to the other neighbor. But they are both brothers, and brothers don't create problems like you other people. That's the way it is for the other houses too. People live one place or another, sometimes to the south and sometimes to the west, depending on the seasons and the degree of relationship. Simple enough, no? Of course, each family has its own home. It's his property, but it's also the property of everybody according to custom. Titles? What titles to the property? No, Monsieur, we don't have anything like that here. No papers, but just listen: we have our word.

"The Elder who died, may the Lord rest his soul in peace, well, he told his three sons and two daughters: you take the roof, and you, you get the wall and a half over there . . . Hey? But no, it's not complicated at all . . . . The ground? What ground? Heavens, it belongs to the community, what else? You build what you want. Private property, all right, but the soil is the soil, and it belongs to everyone. You only have to ask Raho. He knows. He's our mayor; it's his turn this week. Next week, *incha allah*, maybe it'll be me, but I'm afraid you won't have the patience to wait that long."

And time ground up the numbers and words, and scattered their ashes.

Seated facing History, Raho Aït Yafelman contemplated the rising sun. Once he had been filled with their rays of emerald, grenadine, and life. He looked slowly around the village, tumbledown houses the color of earth, doors that opened, silhouettes that went from one to the other, to meet others to wish them good day. He was tired and on the lookout, and his heart was flowing with tenderness. As in every morning, he had recapitulated in his head all the events, in their tiniest detail, that the tribe had had to face since the recent and distant day that it had installed itself on the barren hill, fleeing who knows what famine or what men—already? When you put them all together, from the first to the last, what was their deepest meaning? What was the sign announcing danger? Danger could suddenly look up at a turn in the path that descended straight down to the plain, just as every turn of every minute in time.

Raho knew very well that the resources of the human soul were inexhaustible, and that he and his had used all sorts of artifices and subterfuges one year after another to escape the law of the greatest number and to preserve their peace. But he also knew full well that those were nothing more than the tricks of children, and that inevitably there would come a day when all these mountains would be razed, and then where would their refuge be? He examined the sky. There wasn't a cloud in it. Then the earth. It was parched. The latter had carried generations of the living who now slept in her bosom, and the former had been witness to it all.

Even a short while ago, almost any invader could be resisted (and sometimes defeated by digesting him), any invader who swept through in the name of a god or a civilization or simply in the name of force. Phoenicians, Romans, Turks, Visigoths, Arabs, French, Spaniards, Portuguese . . . . No matter how powerful they were in name and in arms they had faced them because they had come *by themselves.* A single invader at a time when space, and above all the sovereign weather, had undertaken to pacify. Some had remained in the country and had founded families. Others left in search of conquest of less patient peoples. Still others became once again the strangers they had once been. And sometimes, throughout the centuries, there had been felicitous pauses as though humanity had been short on culture, civilization, or religion.

And now? Now no master was alone any more. It was as if, throughout the world, everyone had joined hands to reduce minorities who had somehow been able to survive until the end of the twentieth century to their knees: the masters of money, of raw materials, those of the law, of cruelty and stupidity, the masters of death . . . Some had transmitted their techniques of assimilation, science itself (this jewel of the Occident) became the handmaiden of repression. Faced with this onslaught, without warning, how many seasons could the Aït Yafelman and their brothers hold out?

Raho studies his hands. They were tanned by all of the suns and as lined with worries as his face. He joined his hands, fingers interlaced, and smiled luminously at the evocation of the first day. The fig tree was no bigger than that, only two trembling leaves and some spindly roots when he had planted it in spite of the advice to abandon it and the laughter of the whole tribe. Twenty years later, he raised his eyes and saw the giant shadow of the tree, saw the ripe fruit. Then he prostrated himself, kissed mother earth with full lips and said:

"And when not a bone or a tooth of my people subsists, you will still be here. You, my earth. No one will subdue you. No one will make you die."

With his index finger, he traced the sign of ancient times on the earth, just as his ancestors more than a millenium before had done: a fish surrounded by a star of five branches. The earth would know how to conduct human destiny, if only it were given confidence.

FIRST TIDE

THE PAST

1

Thirteen centuries earlier, in the year 681 of the Christian era, one luminous morning in spring.

Standing on the promontory that overlooks the town of Azemmour at the mouth of the river Oum-er-Bia and the ocean, Hineb looks at the shimmering waters. She hears far off Yerma's clear song and laughter, to which the iron voice of Azwaw answers, like an echo coming from the depths of the water. Nearer to her, as he toddles on a matting in the courtyard of the house, Yassin tries to catch a ray of sunlight with his dimpled little hands and babbles at the top of his voice. He discovered the sound "da" several days ago. It is that syllable that he shouts and repeats in *every* tone without stop, like the trillings of a bird. Already seven months, seven moons. A son. *Her* son. Hineb throws her head back in a gesture of pride. She feels young and full of life. She thanks life.

A pathway bordered with aspens, birches and sycamores descends steeply from the heather-covered promontory. At eye level, it widens and breaks into two directions. One goes toward the village and the port, then continues, paved, to the Jewish neighborhood. The other one goes almost immediately to the fields of barley and spelt. The earth has awakened, Oum-er-Bia has nourished it during its slumber, and the verdure has returned. The cat grass and the rabbit grass, the borage and wort-weed, sweet marjoram, oleanders and morning glories, everything is in full flower under the sun, from the soil of the meadows to the tops of the trees. To the east, where the view ends in the tender green of fields on the side of the slope, is the forest. If there is only the sea to stop it, who has ever known where it begins?

Hineb, who was born on the other side of the Atlas Mountains, is reminded of her childhood perfumed by the resin of cedars and pines that extend off into the horizon. Her father, a Far'oun of the tribe of stone-cutters, spoke of his life in the land of the Pharaohs even more distant, and said: "The earliest men were born in the Orient. Each one of them planted a tree, as a witness to life. That was the Law. It is still the Law." Hineb does not remember if she planted one, or where. Perhaps it was in the land of the Aures, in the faraway time of her adolescence. What she is certain of is that it is a tree right here that gave her two lives: that of Yassin and her own.

She was awakened to the sound of a multitude of cocks crowing, as she was every morning. The town is their domain. Every home has one. Without fail they announce the bloody death of the day star and then its daily rebirth. They set the rhythm of the seasons' development throughout time. They warn of danger. Azemmour owed its survival to them on many an occasion in the past: the plunderers who spring from the desert or the sea are legion. They are killed with shots from slings or with stakes, by arrows and by clubs. Their bodies are thrown from the top of the black cliff into the pit where the waters of the river and of the ocean merge and boil over. Several days later, the fishing is miraculous, but as far back as she can remember, Hineb has never seen anyone kill a cock, not even at the time of the great famine, when drought dealt severely with the territory of the Aït Yafelman, and the Oum-er-Bia herself dried up.

If a rooster dies, it is of old age. His tail-feathers are kept to remember him. Using fibers from dwarf palms, they are woven into necklaces that are suspended at the doors of houses to ward off demons. The one that watches over Yassin's cradle is made of black feathers, as black as the color of hope. Hineb plucked them live, five or six, from the tail of Azwaw's rooster, the day of the birth of their son. In so doing, she had transgressed a centuries-old Law, but Azwaw said nothing. On the contrary, he had smiled.

Azwaw's hand. As soon as she opens her eyes, Hineb's first gesture is to kiss that hand. Instinctively. The man is still asleep beside her on their couch of goat skins. But his hand speaks, even when at rest. It knows how to hold the plow firmly as it opens the earth and rejuvenates it; how to pull the net full of wriggling fish from the river; how to fell an enraged bull; and how to calm the flux of blood in her head when Yerma is ill simply by placing that hand on her forehead. It can deal severely and pitilessly if there is any attempt against the honor of the community and can design the outline of a dike in the sand, or rise into the air at the right moment to approve what the Elders have just said—or to impose silence. It can also . . . oh no!, not caress or massage the nape of the neck, the breasts or thighs of a woman . . . trace on her belly with his fingertips, gently, slowly the contours of the womb, before, to awaken and activate life, and afterward to calm it. At the very thought of it, Hineb jumps out of bed and goes out without making a sound. The fresh air of dawn will perhaps precede once more the heat of the coming night.

On seeing her, the red donkey blinks those eyes of his, fringed with long black lashes. His ears suddenly flattened, he backs out of the shelter and follows her into the dew. She harnesses him to the waterwheel and gives him an encouraging pat on the rump that makes him tremble from his tail to his nostrils. The squeaking noise of the willow-bound buckets as they rise and fall the length of the windlass lasts the time it takes for the woman to go some thirty steps to the House of Fire where the old men and women of the village, each in turn, maintain and renew the embers on the hearth day and night. The donkey has barely done four turns around the well to hoist a full bucket when he stops.

His memory tells him that that is enough for the beginning of this day. No more had been asked of him the evening or the morning before, since the thick-set grass grew up around his hooves. The time was long past when the fields were as red as his coat and when he had to buttress his back legs and pull, pull with all his force to the sound of his master's voice and the cracking of the whip, going back and forth parallel to the long fissure in the soil, furrow after furrow, onto which the crows and other birds swooped down immediately. Even further off in his memory was the time when the sun descended from the sky, inflaming the very thatch of the roofs, drying every gullet and eye. He and his brothers in the enclosure, men as well as women of the village, worked in relays at the seven waterwheels and turned, pantingly turned morning and night, to drag a thin and muddy water from the depths of the earth. Many of his species disappeared that year. If, as a consequence, he had carted away loads of their skulls and their white bones as far as the ravine where the wastes of existence are buried, he still wonders why he did not die of hunger and thirst also. Could he have been too young to be deprived of life? He recalled that the hand of his master had nourished him, caressing his skeletal flanks and striking those humans who approached him with spears and ropes. Then the sun rose again in the sky, clouds covered it, and torrential downpours followed. The climate became once again predictable, dry and bare during the summer season and green the rest of the year.

A tuft of grass between his teeth, the donkey sticks up his ears and distends his nostrils. He turns neither his head nor his eyes. He doesn't even chew. If he is attentive, it is behind him, over there in the house where the master is awakening—and, with him, the little fellow with the strident voice and the young mistress who gambols like a doe. If he inhales, it is in the direction of the fields on the slope of the hill, beyond the river. The scent returns every year at the time of the renewal.

The young mistress with the golden mane no longer mounts him to go galloping off somewhere, at the whim of youth and adventure. She has grown and is taller than her father by a head. All day long, or almost so, they are together, stretching their nets from one bank of the river to the other. At eventide or dawn, they pull them in with white glimmerings and bursts of laughter. Sometimes a sharp whistle alerts him, there where he stands. He has seen it up close, so he knows it is the master's daughter calling him by putting two fingers in her mouth. Consequently, he places himself in the shafts of the cart full of fish and starts out, first in the direction of the section where the Yahouds live, and then toward the storage and drying sheds, where the humans are as busy as bees in a smoking hive. Even more often, he has to go as far as the master's house, situated on the promontory. The path is almost vertical as a tree; it turns and twists, and isn't wide enough for the cart . . .

The deep voice of the master suddenly can be heard, traversing walls and space. Yerma's voice answers, at first slow and indistinct, then clear and lively. Then the two voices become one and change into laughter. The donkey's ears go flat right away: if all goes well, he'll have no work today! Or almost none: to draw two or three buckets of water at mid-day for the master's wife, and three or four others before nightfall. Since she's back in the village, she does not raise her voice as she used to, not even to the master. Now that she has her little fellow, and things are fine, he can live his donkey's life in freedom. Eyes closed, he takes a breath.

The warm odor of humus and seaweed that the morning breeze brings and fills his nostrils comes from both near and far: from the preceding springtime and from his own loins. If he himself recognizes it, if the blood begins to jerk and foam in his veins, swelling them and hardening them, he does not budge an inch. Not yet, not even a hoof. He has time. He is waiting for several things: the return of the woman who harnessed him to the waterwheel, the master who is going to appear on the doorsill soon, and the way he will open his mouth, the quality of his step when he comes toward him, the tone of his voice. You never know in advance with him how a day will go. The donkey had seen many a person flee from Azwaw through streets and fields, or gather around him, at the simple snap of his fingers. That is why he stays where he is, immobile, waiting for the first sign. The grass is still between his teeth. He will only know in an instant if he will be able to calm his blood this day—or put off his joy until tomorrow. Despite himself, the skin of his belly begins to move, run through with chills that are more and more rapid, succeeding each other like the waves of a rising tide.

Hineb, humming softly the song of the warriors, comes strolling along the path. Between two refrains, she blows on the basin full of embers that she carries at arm's length. A white and tenuous ash crowns her hair, rolled into a chignon, with a halo. Her feet are quick; spring is in her voice and life in her entrails, as if, day after day for the seven months since her son was born, she still is giving birth with endless joy.

> Green blood from the mountain, Oum-er-Bia
> Flows and flows and flows in our earth and veins;
> By every drop of water, by every blade
> And shoot of grass, each grain of your sand,
> By all your stones and voices, we swear,
> Oh eternal mother who has brought us here,
> We swear to live forever along your arms
> Throughout the land that you embrace . . . .

When she stops and places the basin on the edge of the well so she can untie the donkey, there is only one thing she stares at: the member of the animal that sways between its legs and beats a tattoo against its belly, as long and gnarled as a cudgel of green oak. There are flames in her eyes at the same instant that she looks at the sex; the fire inside her is stronger and more ardent than all the coals in the House of Fire. It's terrible, this hunger for spasm that she constantly feels since she came back to share Azwaw's couch. She knows that she has already had thirty years of existence, but she also knows that the two years that have just passed have been the true beginning of her youth.

"Go where nature calls you," she says to the donkey. "Go satisfy your ardor until you're exhausted. I'd do just that if I were shut up alone with my man. Day and night, believe me."

The donkey stays where he is without moving on his four feet, insensitive to the tenderness of these words. His shaft slowly rises to half its length, almost grudgingly, and then it descends, turgescent and panting, and begins to sway again. Several drops fall onto the holy earth. Hineb bends down and picks up a stone.

"Go on, I tell you!" she cries vehemently. "Go find your female in heat. Get away from here!"

Things were not always this way. Waves of the past flow into her memory almost every morning . . .

2

One winter dawn, her father had perched her, nubile and slender, on his shoulder. She had awakened with a start as the house where she was born flew into pieces. Her father had lost an eye with the first arrow. Blood ran the length of his neck and onto the hands of the child. Men, with scimitars raised, galloped about on their horses. The wattles of the shacks dissolved with a crash into ruins at the lighting passage of the cavalcade. Roofs, thatch, clay, and dust, all fell to the earth. There was a pounding of horses' hoofs and the terrifying neighing of the mounts, flames flying from their tails. The families of the village, always slow-moving before, all took to flight; uncles, cousins, and neighbors. Some of them did not go very far; their feet were still touching the soil while their heads rolled in front of them, struck off with a single stroke of the sword. The full song of the horsemen, powerful, innumerable, dominated the sound and the fury. Life and death filled all resonant space, sprang from everywhere, rose to the tops of the trees and the mountains, and then fell peacefully back to earth, the earth strewn with cadavers and the dying. Hineb could not understand the words, as it was not her mother tongue, but the emotion was there, issuing from every word of the song, traversing her terror as the light of the sun traverses any cloud. Without knowing why, and despite her suffering and the desolation all around her, she began to weep with joy. Two words had engraved themselves on her mind, while her father bounded, gasping, in the direction of the forest: "*Allah akbar*."

The course of time had reversed itself. At present they slept in the daytime and moved on as soon as night fell: she, her father, and several survivors of the Far'oun tribe. Hineb's mother had stayed behind, perhaps under the debris. They had not a rag or anything from the village. Not even food. Now they ate acorns from the trees, even green ones, sprouts of trees that were blooming, or roots dug from the soil with nails and patience. They drank water from springs or from torrents, even muddy water from ditches. Her father wrapped a poultice of leaves around his head, and his burning fever warmed Hineb's body. The starlit night was an abyss.

At the approach of the fugitives, the Imazighen, other men like them, either ran off or stood up to them. But who were they really? What had they become in their souls? They were greeted in the tribal manner, by tracing on the palm of the hand the sign of ancient times: a fish surrounded by a star. Some faces brightened immediately. Houses, arms, and hearts opened. Tongues loosened and told the news, relating the battles that raged in the country around the Aures Mountains. A being of legend, a young woman whose name was Kahina, had taken the leadership of all the tribes.

Other sons of the earth, Berbers like them through their mothers, fathers, and ancestors, only replied to the ancient greeting with their arms in hand. Far'oun the One-Eyed shouted suddenly: "*Allah akbar!*" It was the password, the key to the new times. He prostrated himself toward the east. Had he not lost an eye in the name of the only god? He, his daughter, and several members of his family went to the other side of the mountain to reconnoiter. Yes, as scouts. It was possible to talk with those brothers as before, after an hour or two of preambles and proper courtesies. The religion of the invaders was no more than a door at which one had just knocked. Once it was open, no one thought of closing it again. It was as if that door had never existed, so timeless were the human relations from one tribe to the other—customs, culture, and mentality deep-rooted in earlier times.

It was these new converts in all good faith, ardent believers if there ever were any, who aided Hineb and her relatives in their flight and their salvation. They knew every tree in the forest, every trap and sentinel, every camouflaged glade where the horsemen of Allah were camped. As they took their leave of their hosts for a night or a week, the Far'oun swore to them that they would embrace Islam as soon as possible. Next year, *incha Allah!*

The Afariks were a totally different type of people. With them, there was neither dialogue nor contact. It was everyone for himself as soon as their presence was felt. They had to be avoided at all cost. They had four limbs, two eyes, two ears, like any other son of Adam and Eve, and a tongue that twisted words and denied the values of the tribe. They had left their own community, to be exact, while remaining on the land and carrying in their veins the blood of their ancestors. They lived by their wits in the country of the conquerors, whoever they were. Romans, Vandals, Christians . . . and Arabs at present. From one generation to the next, they adopted the ways of thinking, the customs, and the laws of the masters who came from foreign places. They had a thirst for power and domination. In exchange, they received expropriated land and some responsibilities of half-masters-half-slaves. That was sufficient to make them feel different from their brothers. They were called the *Ouled el-Bla,* the children of the damned.

Add to that the countless wars, internal and intertribal! They date from the beginning of time, but they took place between brothers, over a woman, a harvest, some cattle, and often for no reason other than the urge to kill. That was the way it was, that was a part of man . . . . The vanquished tribe submitted itself to the conquerors, became their vassal, bore the yoke, and lived in drudgery, until such time as history freed them once again—or were suzerain in their turn. That happened throughout the centuries, wherever there were communities of Imazighen, plains, valleys, and mountains. That was the law. The leaves fell from the trees at season's end, leaving only the trunk and skeletal branches. Then, one day, everything became green and luxuriant again. Certain families, from one war to another, never flourished again, wiped out to the very last person, to the last root. Others, younger and more vigorous, stepped into the gap and perpetuated the race. That was the law of life.

However, no Berber of any tribe had exchanged his skin for a stranger's. Not one had abandoned or denied the age-old tradition to adopt the order or values of the oppressors, except the Afariks. They had lost the most precious possession that a man may have in this world: the ties that unite him with his land. They were no longer the offspring of the earth that had created and nourished them. They were alienated from their community, as though they had rejected their forebears. That is why, alone in the multitude of tribes, they became the instruments of the stranger, docile and efficacious. The partisans of Kahina slaughtered them without mercy, first, in preference to the Arabs who, themselves, did not change the nature of their race, and only carried out their obligations as conquerors.

Between stopping in a grotto in the bed of a dried-up river where Hineb sucked on a pebble to deceive her thirst, and hiding by a thicket high on a mountain pass that was snowy white in the black night, Far'oun talked on about the thousand and one chapters in the history of their people, from the very beginning of the world. He deposited in her adolescent sensibility the secrets of tradition: the names of surrounding living things that can be one's friends or one's enemies according to one's own peace or fear, one's strength or weakness; the significance of the stars that guide one's destiny (this one is warm and beneficient, while that one over there should not be looked at for very long because it rains rays of illness, and that other one, the shooting one, is the presage of a change in your life); the music of the spring-goddesses; the song of the full moon that is the souls of ancestors speaking from their star, and who follow you step by step; the voice of thunder and of the wind; the sense of clouds that are also omens; the soul of the sun; the beneficient earth, divinity of divinities, unsparing with its gifts and its love—and suddenly going dry, becoming inhospitable and hostile because the heart of its sons had dried up previously. And how from the Mother, working within the nucleus of each family, was formed a tribe: by blood.

The women who had procreated, the children who would renew life, and the old persons who were the Elders at the head of the clan, weighted with experience and wisdom, formed the immutable trinity of the tribe. These were the foundations that united its members eternally or else divided them in a few generations if certain principles were not respected: the division of everything among everyone, so equitably that nothing was the property of anyone; the support of each arm in the undertakings of the community; the respect for one's word once given; the law of hospitality of roof, board, and heart; the past eternally present in all circumstances as an infallible witness, in the same way the Elders were witnesses of the tribe; nakedness in the midst of abundance, for who knew what tomorrow would bring? And above all, the cult, not of heroes, but of things accomplished together: a house, a family, a war of defense or of offense, a tool fabricated by several hands, an earthen jar, or a mat.

At the moment that Hineb was about to fall asleep, her father took her in his arms and began to hum. The Far'oun who had escaped the carnage came up to them and formed a circle. Everyone, quietly, almost in a murmur, took up the refrains of other times, as they looked out over the horizon inflamed sometimes by the rising or the setting of the sun, sometimes by the burning fires that ravaged the villages and the immemorial forest: the song of the rain, of sowing time, of harvest, of the spinning wheel, of the cow as she gives birth to her calf, of death and of pardon, of the feast for the baby for its seventh day of life, the meal for the whole village on full moon—so many vocal symphonies composed note by note, strophe by strophe, by each member of the community, the length of generations and of time, and that would never be completely finished. Sometimes the far-distant song of the horsemen of Allah rose far above these familiar words and melodies. Then they fled as fast as they could, and Hineb, running on ahead, could not help but shiver as the tremendous emotion welled up in her body.

"These men are not like any of the invaders of earlier times," her father said to her. "You weep because your instinct dictates it. They may have come to conquer our lands. Surely they have, but also, and above all, to change our souls. Who knows if the god who guides them and drives them from their homeland is good or bad? He is not our god. They say it is the only divinity, but we do not understand: we have no single chief here below. We have several equal, and when one of them dies, he is replaced. Why then should we renounce our beliefs and allow ourselves to be under the control of someone on high whom we don't know, who wasn't named by our council of Elders, and even more important, who is an inhabitant of the sky and not of the earth?

He said to her: "I've lost an eye, but I have the other one to see my way to the end of the trail. You have lost a mother. That's fate. We have no home, no land. Of our tribe, only these few brothers who are with us have survived. But, Hineb, we carry our clan and our village with us and within us. I don't know, and not one among us knows, where our steps will take us or what tribe on the other side of the mountain range will give us hospitality for the rest of our days so that we can knot the thread of our life that has been severed. One day, a son, half you and half the man who will cover you, will come forth from your womb. Until that son is born, you will not cut a single hair of your head. That is the law of patience."

3

Two years of exodus and a long interval afterward.

A man's hand runs up and down the long wheat-colored hair that hangs down to the waist. A round, mature and smiling face, with watchful, comprehensive eyes, with a hint of mischievousness, and perhaps even something of cunning. The half circle of the Far'oun is satisfied and rested. The water of the great river nearby has washed off their dust and their fatigue. Their suffering is over. Everywhere, even on the branches of trees, there are clusters of children, women, and men. They sit silently. They have just heard the story of the long march, and they are thinking about it. They all look at Azwaw and the shadow of his body that dominates and covers the shadow of the young woman with her head lowered. They are waiting to see what he will say. Everything will depend on his first words.

Adobe houses, as thickset as their inhabitants, are solidly anchored to the ground, some built of tree-trunks stripped of bark. Their sheen is like that of the old people who sit immobile on the doorstep, their chins in the hollow of their hands. Sounds of the forge, of metal striking on metal resound as far as the ear can hear; and as far as the eye can see. Hundreds of heads of cattle, muzzle-lowered, graze amid greening fields and flowers of every nuance of life—of desire. Silhouettes fill the eastern horizon with weeding, hoeing, and scything, as far as the forest.

A line of small donkeys led by a red one climbs the length of the steep path. They are loaded with packsaddles full of logs, sacks, and earthenware. No human accompanies them. They know the way. High above, on the promontory, a solitary house watches and protects the town like a lookout post. The orgasmic odor of oil from the wild olive tree couples with the scent of fish and of meat cut into strips and drying in the sun. A few spirals of smoke rise and dissolve in the azure sky.

The lapping of Oum-er-Bia sounds slow and heavy between the river's banks, like blood in the veins of a peaceable man—followed by its roaring at the mouth, like blood bursting from a heart. And water mills. Flat boats

30

with square sails moored to the landing, keels, caressing its side. Others dance on the water. The mouths of the Aït Yafelman are closed, soundless, their faces immobile. A flight of birds with their sharp cry accentuates the human silence. Above Azwaw's shoulder, facing Hineb, is something that she has never seen before, and that envelopes her immediately in its peace: the sea.

"You have cried too much, little one. You have seen too much suffering for your age. That's why your eyelashes have grown so long and are so black. That doesn't go with that sun-colored hair you have. Come on. Lift up your head so that I can look at you!"

Azwaw's voice has not come from his mouth. It rises from the depths of his body, as deep as a well. Hineb is thirteen years old. She is afraid to make a move or even tremble. A calloused finger raises her chin.

"That's just what I said! You can hardly see your eyes. To my mind, you look like that filly I caught with my lasso. The poor little orphan was frightened. And as thin as that! But I tamed her. How's that, you're frightened of *me*?

The rising laughter that shakes him infects the Aït Yafelman, row after row, in successive waves. Far'oun smiles slowly. The survivors of his tribe as well. They nod their heads and look at one another. The battle's won. That's destiny.

"My wife has been dead three days now. It's time for me to remarry. She didn't leave me any offspring. You, little filly, will be my wife. Not right away. Later on. It's no pleasure to cover a bag of bones. You will move into my house from this day on. The women who will watch over you will fatten you up and round out your body in the right places. Is it agreed, father?"

"Yes," replies Far'oun. "Yes, brother, I promise her to you."

"Aha! You were a stonecutter in your native land, from what you told us?"

"Not in my native land. In the land of the Pharaohs, and then in the land of Jugurtha. I was young then."

"You are still young. We'll find a woman for you. There are enough among us. Did you say that houses are built with stones?"

"Yes, houses, and they are solid ones."

"Ours also. We braid switches of green wood, form walls that we cover with clay on both the inside and the outside. It hardens with the sun and with time. How many years would it take you to build a pharaoh's house, for me and my wife and the children she will give me?"

"You want a big house? Then perhaps around summer, if we all work together, the Far'ouns and I."

"Forget about the little one. She can't work. She needs a lot of rest. Let's work through the summer and try for the next season. I'm in no hurry, you understand?"

"Yes . . . I think so."

"There is stone upstream in the river. There are tools for digging it, good bronze tools. And others in a metal I don't know. Ask for what you need from our blacksmiths. There is also an object mounted on wheels—I don't know what it is called—that hauls loads up the hill all by itself, or down. All you have to do is pull on the rope. The Jews built it. It was used to construct dikes and the bridge over there. These Jews brought their science with them in their heads when they fled their own country. One day they came to ask us for hospitality. Like you, right?"

Far'oun says nothing. Although he has never seen a Jew, he has heard the story of their wandering and maledictions.

"They have not mixed with our people because of their beliefs, but they live quietly over there in their own section. They help us and we give them assistance. They are our allies when needed. But you, you are Imazighen like us. We welcome you according to our law. Do you know what that means?"

"Yes."

"The last drop of blood of your tribe will dissolve in our blood, and the descendants, male or female, that come from your loins will be our sons and daughters.

"Yes," repeats the father of Hineb, looking down between his feet. "That is the law of life."

Azwaw goes up to him, stops, and puts his arms around him.

"Do not use sad words, brother. We are Aït Yafelman, which is to say, Sons of the Water. You who speak our language must know that. Look at the river. Where does it come from?"

Far'oun glances up the river then down. He says:

"From the great mountain. We have followed its course."

"Yes, but it cannot survive very long with nothing but its springs. Its tributaries nourish it, numerous streams and rivers that cannot survive by themselves either. Each one of them contributes its water, and if a single stream ceases to contribute its water, the river runs dry. It has already happened."

His voice goes up a pitch, trembling with emotion as he adds:

"It is the same with us, the Aït Yafelman, the Sons of the Water. We are not a single family, but many; not a single tribe, but many. Nevertheless, we form a single community. Each one of us brings his own capacities, his own life experience, his honor and ability in what he knows to do with his hands and what to say with his tongue. But that is enough talk for today. You are tired. Go tear down that house where my wife died and construct a brand new one for me where youth will soon enter. I need it to get married, no? As for the news that you bring us and the dangers that menace our people, we will discuss it all later on at the assembly of the Counselors. We have the time. We need everybody's participation for that."

With thundering laughter, he turns around, walks toward Hineb, and takes her by the hand.

"Come along, you! Let's go eat. . . ."

4

One hot night under the open sky in the patio of the new house that smelled of limestone and lemon, he possessed her. A nightingale was singing. Hineb had undone her chignon, and was crying, without tears or noise, into her long hair that was like a soft veil of silk. Much later, he got up. He was not happy. She had hardly put on any flesh at all. He said in his strong voice:

"What happened to all those good things of life that the women have been stuffing you with? Except for those three little bulges on you, you are still as thin as a cow's tail. How do you expect children to sprout from those narrow flanks, and what would you suckle them with? How do you expect to have the pleasure of a woman when she mixes her ardor with her man's, and he pours his semen into her? . . . . That's why you're upset, eh?"

She was sobbing as he took her on his knees and began to rock her like a child. He said:

"No need to cry! Your eyelashes will still grow, so long that one of these days you won't be able to see. There's no need to hide behind that sunny head of hair and your shame. There is no shame. Look at me: there is no shame! You still don't know the thing, that's all. Certain soils didn't produce anything, not even crab grass. We had to fatten them with mud from the river and the worms it contains in abundance. A year later they were joyous meadows. That's where we bury our dead. Calm down, little filly. You'll soon know my member as you should. Now, calm down, calm down!"

The inflections of his voice were low and slow, like the caresses of his hand. Suddenly, without any forewarning, he became insanely angry. He jumped to his feet and ran into the house. He woke up all the women, relatives and servants, in room after room, and threw them out into the night, interrupting their sleep. If they had contented themselves with an egg and a cup of milk, it was because they were finishing their time on earth, while the young one was just beginning hers. They had no teeth to

33

chew with, no desires, no life, no more nourishing blood. Who would even think of copulating with them except for a lunatic? The meadow was awaiting them, there was still space. Outside! Outside! From tomorrow on he would deal with their tombs, with a good pickaxe. . . .

He spent the rest of the night feeding his anger and stirring up a hellish fire in a cauldron. He prepared for her a dish made of calf's feet, strong pepper, and chick peas.

"Eat! Get some strength for what's to come. Eat to make yourself a woman."

And he covered her in the early hours.

"Aha! That's good fatigue, isn't it? Sleep now, little filly. You won't do anything all day. You eat, you make love with me, and then you will sleep. I won't be back until midday. Rest until then."

Each time he returned, he undressed her and gauged her with his eye, weighed her in his arms, and frowned. After all, the best morsels were for her, shad roe, raw and juicy to the teeth, marrow of wild boar! The honey was up to the rim of the jar, and he plunged his hand into it.

"Here, take this. It's for you. All the juices of our earth are in it."

If she swallowed, it was to vanquish her nausea and her fear, to strengthen her innards. She forced herself to smile. As for him, he said nothing or almost nothing during meals. He ate like four, no matter what, emptying the plates. And after every meal, he took her into bed so that he could see if the food had done its work and seasoned certain parts of her woman's body.

"Come on! Be a woman!"

She feigned pleasure and instinctively cried out like a beast, and once the act was over at last, she would kiss his hand. That hand, that had just caressed her belly to excite her, and that only tickled her. If he wasn't fooled, at least he showed nothing. With his face and eyes smiling, his fury mounted and descended in him like the bellows of a forge. He did not understand. He was kind and gentle with her, he gorged her with food, and even more, he gave her what every woman wants most in the world: the sap of the male. He gave it to her without measure each time that he felt his member rise on him. He held back neither his pain nor his force. And so? And so, another explanation for this dryness had to be found. Perhaps she had lost the creator of her days too early, at the age when mothers communicate to their daughters certain secrets of undergrowth? Yes, perhaps . . . .

He hired a matron, an expert cook and mid-wife. He said to her as he looked her in the eye:

"Dada, you who have so much fat you don't know what to do with it, can you put some feathers on this bird?"

"I can, master. Is there what I need in the house?"

"It's full of victuals. There is even an ox in the shed. Slaughter it if you need to. Take the knife I use to shave the points on the stakes. I sharpened it this morning."

"Tell me about your woman. What's she like?"

"Thin! Thin in front and thin behind. Do you understand?"

"That's too bad! But that's not what I'm talking to you about. Does she have her blood of the month?"

"Yes, Dada. She pays her debt every moon. That hasn't stopped yet."

"There are women who don't have a drop, and that's why they have no appetite. Is she narrow? Is that what worries you?"

"She has no hips, or almost none."

"That's not what I'm talking about. Is she narrow and dry there where you know?"

"That's the trouble, Dada. Come here closer to me, even closer! Dada, she rejects my semen! She does nothing with it!"

"If that's not too bad! I know some herbs, the Souss root, for example. It calms hunger."

"What hunger? I'm just telling you that she . . ."

"I could give you some to calm *your* hunger, master!"

Cooing, she gave him a slap on the back that almost knocked him over.

"Tell me, man: what did your first wife die of? She came to your house plump and left it a cadaver. How did that come about? We've been asking that question for four months now."

"That's something I still have not understood, Dada. She had been having some weak spells for a while, and she had little energy. One night, we were doing . . . you know what I mean."

"No."

"Good. And suddenly she was gasping for air, strangling, and grew stiff, poor thing."

"Poor Azwaw Aït Yafelman! Poor man! Except for your head that is round and your voice that is strong, everything in you is dry as an old man's walking stick. And you are weak, so weak! I'm going to prepare some good little dishes for you that will give you some strength back."

"Get out of here! Go take care of my wife! And don't eat it all yourself. I didn't hire you to blow yourself up to bursting . . . ."

He never did know what bulbs she used to prepare her dishes, or what incantations, roots, or herbs known to women from very ancient times, but thus it was: he was content with every one of them. He was happy with himself, first of all; he was happy with every mouthful whose succulence he savored at length; with the sharp looks that his wife secretly gave him; with the meat that she now ate with a good appetite and that would nourish her own meat there where it was needed. It was a pleasure to watch her walk, sit down, and stretch out on the bed. Her gestures were no longer dry and thin like a faggot, her expression no longer of fear and of meager life in a narrow body. From one day to the next, her gestures became effusive and acquired an easy nonchalance that fascinated him. The shrub of the Aures Mountain had finally become a tree; its trunk grew thicker, the sap rose in torrents. Hineb laughed, she smiled as she listened to him, nodding her head. She looked him straight in the face. She was the first to disrobe, impatient to give him her fever and to receive his heat. When he stretched out on her, by the spirit of the mountains and by the soul of the river, he now had plenty to fill his hands with!

His assaults were still assaults, impetuous and repeated, but curiously enough, he felt them mingled with a kind of peace. If he set out to conquer the body of a woman more than ever, it was by taking his time, with a circumspect approach first of all, and pauses in the course of operations, as if he were counting the strokes as he went along. Strangely, Hineb interested him *even afterward*. He needed her presence. He felt something like a sense of gratitude, without consistency or form, for her. He vaguely wondered why. She was never tired. Stirred by a renewal of energy, she even wanted to get up to do the thousand and one chores that awaited her.

"Later on. Stay here a little while. Rest a bit."

"Rest? Rest from what, my man?" she would ask, in all innocence.

A voice out of the recent past tried to say something to Azwaw . . . just what? It was very indistinct, and became more and more distant and blurred. He adjusted his feelings and his memories for a moment and thought back to his first wife as he tried to make a comparison—and quickly his head would empty itself. Sleep would overwhelm him.

Soon there would be little secret cooings and muffled laughter. Dada was proud of her pupil.

"Did you do what I told you to?"

"Yes. Easily."

"Your heel the length of his back? From the top to the bottom of his spine?"

"Once was enough. That's all."

"Aha! And what did he say?"

"He gave an 'mmmm' as he emptied himself, and then he became very gentle."

"There aren't any children any more," cried Dada as she raised her arms to the skies. "I wouldn't have thought it of you, which just goes to prove that today's young people could teach the old monkey that I am. I have nothing more to teach you, I'm telling you."

"Yes, you have, Dada. A lot, a lot. Tell me other things. Do it for me."

The day Hineb woke up singing, Azwaw thought it was because it was spring. Rays of sunlight inundated the room. Outside, in the patio planted with trees, a flock of birds circled overhead, piped, and sang. His wife was like that. A little nothing amused her, a flower that one could not even eat! He said:

"Ho!"

He took her by the shoulders and shook her.

"Stop acting like a bird. Go light the fire. Me, I'm hungry. Hey! Are you listening to me?"

Her eyes bright, she went on singing, songs from her childhood, of sowing and harvests, the feast day of the tree, which had withered not long ago in her native land and that was reborn in her that morning: all of the clear luxuriant voices of the past. He spoke slowly and in a low voice so that he would not frighten her (she was probably having a nightmare):

"Hineb! Wake up! I'm talking to you!"

He cried at the top of his lungs:

"Hineb! My blood is getting hot. By the demons of hell . . . ."

She freed herself, nimble and bold, and got up without stopping her singing as she looked at him through her long black eyelashes. She was not afraid of him! Nor of the hand he brandished like a hatchet. She dodged it and backed up bit by bit as he moved toward her. Great balls of sweat formed and rolled down Azwaw's cheeks, in the spot where he closed his jaws. He knew that sooner or later he would catch her and that then he would twist her neck in a single motion, from the other side of her head, forever, just as he did with those who betrayed the clan. He would crack the vertebrae at the nape of her neck. But she was his wife, almost a child. And a stranger as well. He ought to warn her before the final gesture. It was for that reason that he stopped, crossed his arms, and by three successive postures let her know that he was truly angry: he looked at her fixedly and harshly; then he bared his teeth and showed them to her; and as she did not seem to comprehend and kept on singing, he went to the final phase, the most terrifying: he began to shake his head up and down.

"Master!" cried a voice pearled with laughter.

He turned around brusquely, short of breath. There was Dada filling the whole doorway with her full body, her breasts thrust forward. She was smiling at him with every dimple.

"You have already taken care of her, the poor little thing, and in such a way. All you still have to do is go choose a calf that you will offer up in nine months, according to tradition."

"What? What are you saying?"

There was as much astonishment in Azwaw's voice as there was joy.

"You have put the time in, Master. It's true that you are already forty years old. Almost an old man. By my faith, I had to give you certain herbs so that your semen would not be still-born."

But he no longer heard the sound of words; he heard only the voice of his blood. He threw himself toward Hineb, took her up on his knee, and bared her stomach which he began to feel with both hands.

"The wonderful little one! So that's why you were singing? From joy? The appearance of these thin little ones, like this one here before my eyes, is deceiving. There's not much flesh, but they're sincere and passionate. I've always known it. Nothing to do with the cows with big udders. Lift up your head. Wipe the blush from your face. It will be a boy," he concluded. "I tell you so."

"Or a girl," added Dada. "Get your paws off from there.

"Or a girl, of course. Of course, but I think it's going to be a boy."

"Get your big paws off. When you put seed into the soil of your garden and it starts to grow and along come some cats that begin to scratch the fresh earth with their claws, what do you do?"

"I throw stones at them, but they usually come back at night while I'm asleep. Then I've found branches of blackthorn. It's full of thorns and prickles. They don't like that. Not at all, but why are you talking to me about seeds and cats right now? That makes no sense."

"Because you would be wise to put some of those branches with prickles into your bed, between you and your wife. She can't chase you away with stones every time you want to approach her. She needs to sleep and let life germinate quietly in her womb. That is the Law."

There was a long silence. Azwaw danced on one foot and then the other. He moved his lips in silence and examined Dada's face and eyes, and those of his wife. Finally he whispered:

"I am not a cat."

"Of course not! Who said such a thing?"

"That law you are talking about with so much saliva doesn't concern the little one. She is not one of ours. She was born on the other side of the mountains. She isn't an Aït Yafelman."

"Oh yes she is! What are you working up in your head? She is pregnant with your child now, and there is no dividing line between her and us any longer. The law of women says . . ."

"Will you shut up! Can't you put a double knot on that dragon's tongue of yours? And you, little filly, don't listen to the silly things that jealous old woman says. She has no man in her bed. That's why she doesn't stop stuffing herself. Better to go light the fire. We've got a good day ahead of us, haven't we?"

"The law of women says that man will not touch his wife from the day that she feels the child move in her womb. That runs the risk of scratching the inside of her womb like a little kitten and of bothering the little one."

Then she added, with a big smile:

"Go on with you, Master. Don't be so sad. You still have four months ahead of you."

"That rotten law of females isn't one I voted for in the council. Not me! Never. Not my dead father or my ancestors or any other members of the tribe."

"But your mother voted for it, and your grandmothers."

"I wasn't there. You know very well that there are women who continue to accept their husbands up to the time of the labor."

"I know some. They're all selfish, a savage tribe that lives on the other side of the river, not Aït Yafelman. Have you seen their children? Skinny and full of sickness. Most of them don't live more than two or three years."

"I don't like the law. It's an animal law, or amounts to the same thing. We walk on two feet."

"Women do too. That's why we're represented on the Second Council, as equals with the men. From one year to the next, we put the law passed down from mothers of time immemorial through again. Thanks to it, we have strong children. Look at yourself and look around you. I'm surprised, Azwaw, son of your mother, that you aren't the first to defend us. After all, you are our leader. You've been elected by two councils."

"There is no leader. You haven't understood at all."

"It's true that before you there wasn't any. I remember well, son."

Azwaw breathed through his nostrils. He had arisen expecting a good day, as the harvest was going to be good. But then he had let himself be caught up in words. He had been wrong to listen to them and to answer. He said:

"I was elected to carry out the decisions taken by the Elders after the deliberations of the Council. I am simply an agent. You're starting to burn my ears."

Dada shook her head in commiseration. Her multiple chins shook with silent laughter.

"Oh yes! Oh yes, nothing but a poor agent! You don't do anything more than speak for the Elders. To such a point that the ones who don't have a voice, the ones who are so old, well, you lend them your voice. And the ones who can't walk you carry on your back to the House of the Council. You kill yourself doing service to others, often in spite of what they themselves want, because that is your nature. From the covered bridge to the salting of fish, as well as the branding of animals and the guard duty, what doesn't go through your hands! Blessed Azwaw!"

For a moment Azwaw spoke with his head, in every possible direction. He did not get the expected response. Very calmly he said:

"We could pretend that nothing about that old law has been said within these four walls, right? We'll talk about it again when my son is of voting age. When that time comes, we'll be a majority because there will be one more man in the village, and you, you won't be in this world any more. So what do you think about that?"

By way of answer, she smiled from one ear to the other.

"Good," he continued beyond the calm of what is called reason. "We could act as though I didn't know a thing. As though no one had said a word to me. No one has told me that my wife is pregnant by me. You can't even see it. I'll be told about it the day that I hear cries of pain. Hineb doesn't know what state she is in either. This is the first time this has happened to her and so how do you expect her to make comparisons? She has just begun to taste the good things of life. Isn't that right, little filly?"

Without sounding one note higher than the next, Dada said:

"The little filly has two ears, and at the hour we're at now, they are full of my words. She knows what the mothers' law of ancient times means. Women are like that: they never forget anything."

"I wonder why I ever brought you into this house!" he cried in a single outburst.

"So that your wife will be a woman. Are you happy with your servant, Master?"

"No."

"But you're happy with the idea of being a father?"

"No. You have spoiled my happiness. My wife's, too, the poor thing. A while ago she was singing with happiness, and just look at her now. Look what you have done. Like a rat up against the wall, seized with terror."

"A few minutes ago, you wanted to kill her because she was singing."

"That's my business! Go back to that hurly-burly head of yours, and do your *feminizing* and *venomizing* somewhere else. There's sunshine and wind outside. Go out and air your blubber."

"Yes, Master. I'll go down to the port to announce the good news."

He looked at her as if seeing her for the first time. Without a word, he stepped boldly out into the morning sunlight, thick-set, solid, the master of his life. He would do what had to be done once the moment arrived. He had eternity in front of him. Night gave way to day, the earth renewed itself and rejuvenated itself from one springtime to the other, the river added its life to life. Only man, the son of the soil, accepted the process of aging, in his body and in his ideas. All of man's existence was nothing more than a series of wanderings between two voids: the one from which he came and the one to which he would return one day. No one he knew, with the exception of himself, Azwaw, had had the courage to confront the past, to raise up the tombstones.

He was only thirty years old when the Council named him speaker for the Elders: his cast-iron voice had a deep resonance that carried very well. The city was directed at that time—directed!—by the censer-bearers of death, all priests of different gods, enemies of one another and, above all, of man. There was the dragon-god of the river to whom small infants were sacrificed to quiet the devastating floods; an earth goddess for whom living virgins were buried alive every time there was a severe drought; an ocean divinity to whom the infirm and the lunatic were thrown; gods of wind, of thunder, of the blackness of night, of rain . . . . Twelve gods whose priests Azwaw had taken out in his big boat one beautiful evening into the estuary of Oum-er-Bia, out to a whirlpool known only to him. He had acted in such a way that it had to be they who decided the emplacement of the future dike. Several of them tried to swim. He split their skulls open with his oar. He told the assembled council, soaking wet and trembling from head to toe:

"The Dragon-God of the river swallowed up every last one of them and consumed their bodies down in the depths. There won't be any more flooding. He let me escape to carry out his orders. Here they are . . . ."

Two or three season later, he had placed his own men in key positions, people of his own blood: brothers, cousins, relatives of different degrees. And he became the master of Azemmour. The Council of Elders and of the women were still there. That was traditional. Their members still had full powers, palavered and decided in words. It was Azwaw who acted.

"A little while ago, why were you singing, Hineb?"

"I don't know, Dada. Just singing, no reason."

"Aha! You are going to be taking care of your little one instead of your husband. Isn't that it?"

"A little bit. Yes."

"You didn't feel anything, did you? Despite the concoctions that I gave you to drink at night?"

"Not much of anything, Dada. I'm bad, bad!"

"No, you aren't, my little one! Not at all! Quiet yourself. Dry away those tears. It's springtime in your womb. Do you know what you're going to do when your child is born?"

"No. I know nothing of life."

"You will give him your breast as long as you can, even when his teeth start to come in. As long as you give him your milk, you will be more mother than woman. The rest will follow automatically. Do you understand?"

Hineb, head down and lips shaking and shivering, said nothing.

"You are still sad, little one?"

"How much longer will it go on? These lies, this . . . this fear that I feel inside myself?"

"As long as your woman's body has not spoken for itself. But that time will come. Yes, that will come. Tell me something: the way you have just asked me that question makes this old lady perk up her ears. You've ended up with an attachment for your man, haven't you?"

"From the very first day when . . . he caressed my hair. He is good."

"He's the only one who doesn't know it. Talk to me more about him. Go on. Speak up."

"He is as strong as the cedars of my native land. I can count on him."

"That is what we all feel. When he puts an ox to the plow, it isn't the animal that pulls. It is Azwaw who pushes. The city has exchanged the shadows of night for the light of day when he took our destiny in hand, just one generation ago. *You are his only weakness.*"

She took Hineb in her arms and whispered into her ear:

"Give him a son. During every moment of your pregnancy, month after month, you must think, more and more strongly, that you are going to give birth to a son. And it will be a boy. We'll have need of him one day, when Azwaw leaves this life."

It was a daughter. He brought a heifer into the room, pushing it with all his strength. He cut its throat right there. Then he wet his finger in the frothing blood and traced the sign of ancient times on the new-born baby's forehead: a fish surrounded by a star.

"I call you Yerma in the name of the earth and the name of Mother Spring. Today is a day for joy. Long, long life to you, Yerma!"

And then, calm and smiling, he no longer left the house. Day and night, his steely eyes remained riveted to Hineb's breasts. Once he was sure that there was no milk in them, not even a drop, he did what he had to do: he repudiated her. There and then, without explanations or regrets.

She was worthless now, so he let her go wherever her dry little destiny might call! He wanted nothing to do with illness, whether of the body or of the mind. He easily replaced her with a generous wet nurse—and a goat with swollen udders, just in case.

5

One luminous morning in the year 681, Yerma was standing in the river. The water, up to her knees, was flowing slowly as it sang its way between her legs. There, in front of her, is a white rock, on which she beats clothing rubbed with wood ash. Each time that she raises the cloth-ing to smack it back down against the rock, a shower of droplets sprays all about her in a rainbow tinted by the rising sun. As she is standing, her arms are bare to the shoulders, her linen dress lifted, its straps tied around her neck. Rose-colored flamingos, motionless, except for their beaks which pry into the mud or nuzzle into their ruffled feathers, are almost within touch of her hands, there on the bank among the furze. And, in the middle of the river and in the sky, are the legions of gulls, small crows with scarlet bills, and black birds with yellow wings whose names she does not know.

Then, from behind her on the other shore, she clearly hears the voice of her father, standing upright in his boat. From sheer pleasure she does not turn around. Jokingly she cries out:

"I can't hear you. You're too far away!"

"Hey-ho! Yer-ma! I'm coming clo-ser! Hey-ho!"

An oar plunges into the water, cutting it with a sound like a fin. Yerma still does not turn around, as she continues to beat the clothing. Without her realizing it, her gestures become more rapid and as irregular as the flow of her blood.

"Who are you?"

"Me!"

"Who's that, me?"

"*Khoukhoublaà!*"*

"What do you want of me?"

"There are a lot of fish, a lot. I can't catch them."

"Why can't you, *Khoukhoublaà?*"

---

*Untranslatable. This is an affectionate term to frighten children—and to make them laugh—when you tell them fairy tales.

"I have forgotten the song of fishing."

"I have too. Go your way. I don't know you."

And, by irresistible notes and scales, mouth closed, she hums and then sings, with all her might, the sacred song of her childhood—a childhood illuminated night and day by the voice of her father, the look in his eyes, the warmth in his hand. *Li-la-la-la-la-li-la-la-la-la-la!* . . . All the words of the tribe are out-of-date. She could no longer keep silent: *Lo-lo-lo-la-la!*

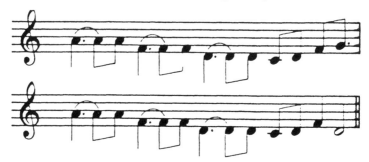

How old was she when her father took her out to fish for the first time? The tiny hands grasped the big thumb with all the strength of joy. He said:

"Yerma, my light of the moon, I am going to tell you a secret. The fish is there, down at the bottom. You have to speak his own language to him so that he will come up to the surface and let you catch him. Do you understand?"

"So you know him, do you, Papa?"

"Of course I do, but the fish are so afraid of my big voice. Who knows why? They'll listen to you and strain their ears, because you have honey in your voice."

She repeated the song and the words and learned it by heart. Then when she sang the song of the fish and saw Azwaw hoist the woven net wriggling with silver fish, she believed in him truly. Still now, she half believes that the human voice can do anything: darken the sky or make a deer eat out of the hollow of your hand. Everything depends on the sounds that rise from the heart to the lips.

That very day, Azwaw bit off the head of the first fish he caught by the tail. He gave the best parts to his daughter: "Eat while it is still alive. Let the soul of the river enter your body and communicate its eternity. Eat, my light of the moon." He satisfied himself with the leftovers. He spit out the bones and the innards with a laugh. It was the first blessed morning. That one was followed by hundreds of others. *Li-la-la-la-la-li-la-la-la-la-la!* . . .

Lo-lo-li la! Lo-lo-lo la-la! . . . . She stops between two refrains and listens. Behind her, she hears the slapping sound of an oar in the water, the voice with bronze inflections, the creaking of the boat as it glides along, and the rustling of the sail ballooned out by the wind that comes from the sea. She still does not turn around: all of the noises will soon die down because someone very much alive is going to come forth, take her by the waist, and hold her in his arms. Then, when she raises her eyes toward her father's face, she'll be unable to say anything, not a single word, won't even be able to smile for the adoration that has filled her heart to bursting, for fourteen years.

That morning at the end of the seventh century and of a thousand years of history, Azwaw was incapable of reaching his daughter. He could not even get near her, in spite of all his strength and his mad fury. Between him and her, a human being who had already known two types of death died this time for good, in the tranquil Oum-er-Bia, pronouncing without being conscious of it the first radiant word of a famous surah of the Koran . . . .

The first memory of Yerma is a pair of jaws in movement, jaws covered with hair. Above them were two holes of black tenderness: the eyes of her father that she had always seen open. Even at night when she cried or tossed in her sleep, a flame with an odor of tallow cut through the darkness, and the warm eyes were there, and the hand and the reassuring voice.

As far back as his memory of more than half a century goes, it is always a little girl full of life that Azwaw sees: he sets her balanced on his knee and she sways a bit and looks attentively at him as she waves her little arm impatiently with joy. When the food has been well chewed and salivated, he uses his thumb like a spatula to set aside small portions that he puts between the open lips of the child . . . nuts, berries, barley, bread, fish, meat, goat cheese. Water is easier to handle, as is milk and honey: directly from one mouth to the other. For a long time he slept wearing the only lichen-colored smock he had because Yerma's greatest pleasure was to fall asleep with her little hand, whose thumb she was sucking, holding onto the collar of that very smock . . . .

If Azwaw thinks about the war that is spreading everywhere and getting nearer, it is to chase it out of his mind . . . tomorrow! He has taken precautions for the city, woven a series of defenses to which even former enemies, the tribes of the area and from beyond the plains and mountains, contribute their feline cunning and their deadly bravery. Tomorrow he would apprise the Council of the situation, with the emissaries he had sent out more or less everywhere, the *rekkas** he had sent out toward the far horizon. He may present them tonight, if they are back and if Yerma sleeps quietly again, but it is not certain. She has just cut her first tooth.

The war is still far away in space and probably in time. These invaders are only human, after all, like the Romans, the Phoenicians, and the other conquerors who preceded them. They could well be exterminated and digested to the last man, they and their horses, who knows? If unluckily they got this far, well, it would be ten years off, or fifteen, or twenty. He knows the Imazighen and their souls steeped in savagery through combat.

---

*Foot emissaries, capable of traversing every imaginable terrain and of breaking speed records. Several types of these "ambassadors" still exist.

Their attachment to the Mother Earth is the same as his: fibers, nerves, blood. No one in the course of centuries has been able to reform them, not even "for their own good."

Yes, they would do whatever they could to slow the approach of the horsemen from the east as long as possible. He had given them pledges and had sent them his best officers. From now until then, he, Azwaw, would have the time to save his people, or at least the time to preserve their patrimony in case of calamity and until the end of eternity. From now until then as well, this burgeoning life that is there before him, bursting with health and juices, would have the time to walk on its two legs, to grow up, and to run, and to have all its teeth, to become a true woman of the earth according to the traditions of the Aït Yafelman. If she came forth one day from a dried-up chicken womb, he would know how to form her womb, with his own hands, so that she would be a source of pleasure for herself and for her man—and give birth to sons and daughters, full of life, to take the place of earlier generations.

He knows that every being must inevitably weaken and die, just like any tree, no matter how deep its roots. But he also knows that his own existence has consisted of not letting himself be vulnerable to what those priests he drowned called destiny, and never to fall prey to words or ideas. *He does not know destiny.* That is for others. He only asks two things: that there be several days in every day, and two or three lives in a man's life so that he and his can become once more what they originally were: everything. In the measure of the earth and the dimensions of time. Without words and without thought. The history of the first men has been transmitted down to him and others like him, from generation to generation.

Sometimes he goes to look for Oumawch, the *amdyaz,* the ancient blind bard, and installs him near the hearth. Oumawch also knows. He is the eldest of the Elders, ageless. In the Council, he says not a word. He listens. Then, a week or a season later, he shares with Azwaw his thoughts, even as he apologizes for himself.

"Tell me, Oumawch! Tell the story of our ancestors with your poetry. Tell the little one how and who they were. She is old enough to learn now."

Oumawch has a long-bow, but he has never shot an arrow, only two notes, one solemn one followed by a shrill one, always the same, without end. And perhaps without beginning as of the moment he sounds them. The bowstring is stretched to its limit. He plucks it with his thumb and index finger, and the resonances that result from it echo in his memory and awaken thoughts of the past. Women, men, and a flock of children who followed him to the house of Azwaw (a compact and interchangeable group accompanies him to every dwelling in the city) now sit in a semicircle and wait with their hands on their knees and their faces frozen. They do not look at the blind man with the white hair, nor at his hands nor those of the person next to them—at neither things nor persons. *They look at his voice,* as rough as the rocks of the mountain, broken at times like the ocean, that narrates and then sings.

The curtained screen of sleep and dream
closes behind my sightless eyes,
and now the veiling of another time
of this world's first day, is lifted,
day that our present men and all of those
who preceded them in ages past
kept hidden by the shadow of their words . . . .

He pauses an instant and then goes on playing the same interminable notes, more and more rapidly. There he is, very fragile, almost without substance, his head turned to one side, surprised not to hear the sniggering that usually concludes the first strophe of his poem of the world.

"Go on, Oumawch!" says Azwaw. "He is not there. Go on in peace. He has left."

Children, women, and men repeat with one single voice:

"He has left. Go on, *amdyaz!*"

No one tells anyone what it is all about: if *he* has left, *he* has left. That's the way it is. That's life. Oumawch shakes his head and holds the solemn note, repeating it seven times. Then he sounds the sharp one, one time. He says:

"My mother told me this a long, long time ago. And my grandmother had told it to my mother, and so it was from generation to generation through time. That way our story has not been lost. I am going to recount to you the true History: that of the Earth. Then I will tell you how the History of men who have taken up so much space afterward and made so much noise and wind, that bit by bit has replaced the History of the Life-giving Mother, effacing Her like a discolored garment, took the form of *legend.* Now sing, my music, sing! . . . ."

He stretches the string of the bow a bit more and makes it vibrate to the limit of hearing. He sings:

At the beginning of all there was the Earth.
Above her, around her, there was nothing at all.
In her breast, several lives existed,
above her, around her, shadows and cold.
There were seven periods, seven creations:
She gave birth to the first of her children.
To give warmth to the world: the sun
that, in its turn, had numerous descendants: the stars.
She created, by turn, the inhabitants
between Earth and sky: the birds
to assure until time's very end
the life of the sun and the stars.
In the course of the third epoch, she gave,
because all above her, around her, the world was all dry.
Yes, she abundantly gave her milk:

the waters of springs, of the issafen,* *of seas and of clouds....*

He pauses once more and listens. The voice that usually contradicts him is not heard. Neither word nor laughter. Azwaw gets to his feet and offers the old man a jug of milk and a handful of dates. He says:

"Drink and eat, man of inspiration. Gather strength to bring the paradise of other times to life again. The man will not return."

Everyone exclaims: "Never again."

If Azwaw believes in the creation of the world in the way that Oumawch explains it and has sung it all along, it is because his own mother told it to him a thousand evenings in almost the same words, but maternally. He was a small boy. She was a simple woman. In order to resuscitate the distant times, she used a *bendir*: a hoop of wood on which she had stretched and fixed the skin of a freshly killed kid. Before she ran her fingers over it, she heated it on top of hot coals until a single note emanating from the center of the *bendir* released an infinity of echoes. She closed her eyes, like a blind person, and let herself be guided by their throbbings and their resonances to find the word, the rhythm, and the emotions of her childhood—and of her ancestors. Often she would cry and could not go on. And each time it was as an older woman, much, much older, who remembered and who burst into tears. Then she would say: "tomorrow." She had been dead for a long time, but her presence endured. Azwaw knows that as he listens to the voice of Oumawch, it is above all the voice of his mother that he hears. It was she who taught him everything, from hunger to thirst for life.

The fish of the rivers and seas to suckle the water of the Earth; the flesh that this same Earth has given in the form of greenery, of trees, of fruits, and of animals, to provide sustenance for what She has engendered; the marriage of all her preceding creations (animals, greenery, water, birds, sun) to form man and woman; and, finally, the seventh period that has just begun: that of the balance of all the offerings of the Beneficient Mother—yes, certainly, yes! Azwaw would like to have faith in what has happened to him in this final part of the seventh century, simply because the creator of his days had told it to him as she beat on the *bendir*. But his mother was no longer of this world, and his ancestors, whom he would so like to resemble, even less so. She and they may have had the luck to live closer to the dawn of creation. He himself is a witness: this century is disconcerting beyond expression, cruel and terrible, and he must face up to events and relegate beliefs to a secondary plane, and act in a way that keeps his community alive.

The dike of the Oum-er-Bia was built by him to contain the floodings. The river did not do it! The portcullis of stakes driven into the open sea, to eviscerate the feluccas of the invaders coming from the other side of the horizon, was also done by him. It was his work, not that of the gods. It was he and not the Elders who had forged and joined the inhabitants of the

---

*Plural of *assif* (river).

city. In earlier times, they had formed three clans within the same tribe: sailors, farmers, and shepherds with their flocks, strangers one from the other, each with his own territory within the same territory, without either sharing or pardon. And, within each clan, there were caste divisions, from the warriors on down to the paid mourners and grave diggers.

Azwaw's mother, unspoiled and pure, was the servant of a priest of who knows what god. She was dying of hunger. She nourished herself and her children with the legends of earlier times. Recently, as he was turning the soil of a fallow field, Azwaw saw her again under the great sun of summertime: some bones. She was still wearing her necklace of cock feathers.

Oho! No! He says nothing to anyone about what he is thinking, nor about what he has done or expects to do. If he talks at all, it is to himself in the darkness of night before he goes to sleep. Later on, when his daughter is no longer of an age for games, he will recount to her his life. How often he had foreseen the catastrophe of words! He knows that many tribes, once vigorous, broke up because they rested on their past glories. And not simply tribes, but whole peoples: Romans, Phoenicians, Greeks, and Egyptians . . . whose bards now tell the story, truly both beautiful and sad.

"Speak, Oumawch! My kidneys are aching from digging. Make me dream."

Far'oun, after all, did not react any other way. If he brought about contradictions, if he sneered as he listened to the history of the Earth, it is because he loved the earth. He knew it. It was his profession: the cutting of stone. He left life, feet first. Or rather, head first, poor one-eye! He wanted more than anything to construct a granary of stone. People tried in vain to reason with him and to explain to him on his right side (on the side that he had his eye), with very simple words, that the country of Egypt that heated his tongue was way off over there, far off in the distance, and that it was inhabited by the Misriyine,* and that they could do what they wanted to according to their own customs! Their *assif* was bordered by sand and rocks, from what was said, and not by fields and forests.

They, the Imazighen, had always stored their grain between a thatched roof and a second ceiling of reeds. The community's silos, three or four of them, were constructed as follows: with trunks of trees blown down in storms and masonry for the foundations; reeds of the Oum-er-Bia and thatch for the rest of it. There was plenty of material, so why dig and raise masses of great weight, utilizing the Yahoud's machine mounted on wheels? What field mice? What rats? Those gnawers have to eat something too! Alright for a dike or a small fortress, or a house, if absolutely necessary, but why imprison (for years) the fruits of grain fields in that sort of tomb where they grow moldy? Far'oun could not give up his idea. He wanted to bring what he "scienced" as the . . . the what then? Oh yes, the

*Egyptians.

"civilization of the Pharaohs and the gods."

It was difficult to talk with a stranger and with a brother even less. And everybody knows that a person with one eye sees bigger and farther than someone who has two. A great stone block that he was cutting down by the river's edge fell on top of him and flattened him out in the riverbed. They were both left where they were: the stone was too heavy to move, and the man was dead.

It is on this white rock that Yerma will one day do her washing as she sings the song of fishing. She did not know about this. She had not known her grandfather, nor had anyone told her of his existence. Not even Dada. Orders are orders.

Dada is not dead yet, but her death is not far off. That is what Azwaw thinks as he watches her turn around and around in the house as she searches, ant-like, for little tasks to do. The wet-nurse had done her job, and so he told her to leave. As a gesture of thanks, he gave her the goat: she no longer had any milk herself.

But Dada stayed on. He had told her to leave, and she would have done so, but she didn't know where to go. She was full of good intentions: she was attached to the master and to the place and . . . yes indeed, she wanted to take care of the girl, Yerma! Azwaw looked at her without saying a word, looked at her once. Since then, she has permission to take care of the little one when Azwaw is called away for some catastrophe in town or when he has pressing things to do. As he only responds to her hubbub of words with a monosyllable ("Oho!" "Aha!" "Eh?" "Eyyeh?"), she has begun to talk to herself morning, noon, and night. Sometimes she talks to objects and animals: the earthen cooking pot, the linen chest, the broom that she takes from room to room, the red donkey that beats its sides in the courtyard. She has to do something, but she has nothing to do, or so little: preparing meals, walking on tip-toe and moving about with a minimum of noise. Azwaw watches her with sharp eyes and laughs up his sleeve. He loves to study human nature.

Dada is still a member of the Second Council, but other women, younger and fresher, have become a part of it—more sensitive to the matters of men. And then a Third Council was constituted: that of the active members of the village. Was this through Azwaw's influence? He doesn't even know himself. He had just expressed the idea that, if the Elders bring the voice of their experience and their wisdom to the community, and if the women represent the future that they have procreated, then it would be desirable to be able to freely express the toil of the men who were neither elderly nor female. Without attracting too much importance to it, he added: "In that way, they will be neither with us nor against us in case of adversity. They would obey your decisions as elder persons more spontaneously, as they will have the feeling of being your equals."

And he said nothing more. He left it to the others to take their responsibilities. That came about without too much difficulty: two or three months of words and haggling. The Third Council was formed—the humblest in outward appearance, but the most active in the background. If the majority of its members were lieutenants, men in the palm of Azwaw's hand, that was not his doing. More than ever, he is the spokesman of the Three Councils. He is simply the executor of their orders.

Yes, the gravedigger will soon dig a tomb in the new cemetery near the port. Dada has good need of it, doesn't she? She is a widow without descendants, although she has helped many women give birth and deal with their men. But no one asks for her services anymore.

Some rumors that Azwaw doesn't want to hear have spread through the village. He pays no attention to the details. He remembers, of course, that Dada stood up to him one day in front of Hineb. But that was a long time ago! He carefully watches this woman who moves her lips, too old and too leathery to interest a man any more, and who, from morning to night, circulates throughout the house, from the rooms to the patio and from the patio to the courtyard. Just what is she looking for? She nibbles all day long, laughs without a sound, and invents dust and cobwebs. He once attached her to the plow to really give her something to do—and to give a little rest to the ox—but she melted in sweat and tears after a single afternoon. He knows that what she really needs is not company or conversation, but solitude. Certain individuals are like that: as twisted as *sedras,** prickly even with themselves and incapable of giving the smallest fruit. Better to get rid of them right away, but they don't let themselves be killed easily. Too many thorns, and roots as hard as rock.

If Dada does not stop washing away at things all day long, ladling water as though the baby could not stay wet for the duration of a chicken's cluck, he knows why: she is searching for the sap that never flowed in her veins. And the sap's vigor, from earliest youth on, is maturity. As everyone knows, that is as true for trees and for rivers as it is for human beings. Certain tribes never reach maturity, no matter what their acts or words. That is why they disappear in the holes of memory, like forgotten dreams. It only takes some unexpected event (an invasion of locusts, a typhoon, an epidemic, a flood, or some other calamity) to know who is good and who is bad, who feeds on life and who cultivates death. It is at such moments that the true nature of human beings is revealed. Azwaw has verified this many times. No, careful, he has no confidence in two-legged animals. When houses burst in abundance, their inhabitants look at you with their souls, and then, when drought comes, there is no more soul or even sight. It was like that the year the Oum-er-Bia dried up . . . .

---

*Shrubs made up exclusively of black thorns, as long and sharp as daggers. Even hunting dogs do not go near them.

6

There was scarcity everywhere, and fever that seized a man on his feet and made him black all over, with knots at the back of the neck, and that felled him before your eyes in a day's time. For Dada, there was something even more serious: the lack of water. What could she wash with? Azwaw attached her to one of the city's waterwheels, as he did for all the Aït Yafelman, turn by turn, including the children. The children were thirsty too.

"No washing!" If you want something to drink, you work at the noria. It's that simple. Maybe you'll bring up a bit of muddy water from the bowels of the earth, and if ever you 'wash up' whatsoever with a single drop of that water, I'll turn you over to the people whose lips are taut with hunger. The flesh of an old woman can be eaten, can't it? Blood can be drunk. Go on and turn the wheel and go on living. Turn with your mind full of prickles and thorns!"

It was ludicrous to watch her panting away, with her skin ever more flabby and drooping around her body like an old blanket. He expected to see her fall dead on the spot, truly, but she survived. She helped to bury the others, younger than herself and with far more to hope for. She resisted famine, fatigue, and the black death—she resisted it all, even herself. Certain sedras were already there before the tribe, waiting. They would survive her.

It was a time of renovation. And then . . . and then, time overlapped time. Summer came in the midst of spring and lasted for several seasons. The springs throughout the south of the country went dry as soon as they appeared. Some people said the same for the west and the north, beyond the mountain range. So cooked and recooked was the earth that it crackled under one's footsteps. From morning until nightfall, day after day, the sun shone white and radiating. At night, the heat was like that of a hot coal. And back it came the next day, and the day after. No wind, not even a sea breeze, or as fleeting as a breath. Blasted the flowers and the buds from the first noonday. Scorched the barley and the wild oats. The thatch of roofs burned with a thick, acrid smoke. Lizards shriveled up in their holes, and insects while in flight, and the yellow grass; and all the trees, even the centuries-old cedars, lost their leaves. The eternal river trickled leanly, with its last few drops of water, like a mother exhausted from suckling a child. Then it dried up completely.

Blood gasped for breath in people's veins, and fear hardened in their hearts, and in turn revealed itself as courage. Scores of people, weakened by hunger and thirst and then struck by the black fever, even the Yahoud, fell to their death. Medicines that once had been so effective were useless. With a single strong voice, they begged for mercy from their two gods, Yhw and Moussa, and a third whom they implored to come to them, a certain Missah. "*Ya wili! Ya wiliwili!* . . . ." They scattered ashes on their heads and tore open their cheeks with their fingernails. "*Ya wili!* . . . ." The sound of their prayers, shrill and overpowering, rose from the port area, obliterating the agony of the living and the jolts of the carts that carried the dead, to the trot of donkeys, to the cliff.

Someone nails a red cloth to the door of their house to warn that the sickness has entered there and that no one should come near. Then another appears a little bit farther on, and then another, from one section to the next. The whole city reverberates to the sound of hammering as one day melts into another. That is Azwaw's law. On the very first day, he had his men set fire to a house, and its occupants, where a dead body had been concealed. A cadaver can contaminate the living, and Azwaw does not like death. As the example was not sufficient, he gave the order to burn the whole area. They did so. They obey only him. He had placed them in key positions a long time earlier, as a provision against certain calamities of heaven or earth. Coming out of the shadows, they are now on a work footing, a group of determined young people who fear nothing. They are called the Watchmen. Azwaw distributes rations of clear, cool water to them. Only he knows the hiding place, foreseen years in advance.

"It's water fallen from heaven, isn't it?" he asks them with a smile of sarcasm.

He is everywhere at once, even in places where he is not. He stands entirely naked, with his body smeared up to the eyes with a mixture of clay and wild olive oil to protect him from the sickness and to permit him to slip through the fingers of any possible assailant. He has strings wrapped around his wrists so many times that they are like bracelets. At the end of each string, there is a little ball of iron, apparently of no significance, but he only needs to move his arm and the string unwinds. Then the ball flies free, powerful enough to crack open a skull like a ripe melon. It is a gift from Moushi the rabbi, the head of the Yahoud tribe.

Yerma sits piggy-back on Azwaw's shoulders. She too is naked and covered with a kind of gray paste that fits her like a second skin. She is nine years old and inseparable from her father, whether day or night. She knows that nothing can happen to them, to her or to him, as long as they are together. It is at that time that they begin to sleep in the same bed.

In the early morning, a door opens and quickly closes, as if with reluc-tance. A body, swollen by the heat of the night, lies on the threshhold. Wolves, hyenas, and jackals that have come out of the forest wail loudly. They surround the city, despite the watch fires and the fire-brands that are thrown into their eyes. They become bolder every day and come closer. More starving than the other animals, the dogs, grown wild because they no longer have masters, soon begin to attack. With stones and cudgels, the Watchmen fight packs of hounds for the dead bodies, before throw-ing the cadavers off the top of the black cliff into the ocean. They often need to take cadavers from humans as well, as the need for meat super-cedes all notions of humanity. They would eat their own mother.

For Azwaw the famine was a benediction. He said to the Watchmen: "Give the dead to these animals that are barking. After all, they are hungry."

He placed each of his men in the suitable place for a gigantic ambush. There were plenty of clubs, stakes, and pitchforks. And little patience. He gave a brief order: "Kill!"

Later on, he assembled the tribe in the main square, examining the crowd with a sharp eye. Then he said slowly and softly:

"There is some good meat to calm your hunger and warm blood to slake your thirst."

Then he bellowed: "Don't touch it!"

Using a whip, he formed *rezzous* then and there, hunting commandos that he drove ahead of him into the forest, each man dragging a body by the feet as a kind of bait.

"Now go to it! Chase the jackals and the wolves! See to it that they don't eat you. Earn your keep, or hunger will twist your bodies and thirst will strangle you! Life is a question of life or death, nothing more, nothing less."

And he placed the Watchmen in a cordon the whole length of the border of the forest, ready to jump on the fugitives at the first sight of so much as the tip of an ear, overcoming their fear and becoming once again Aït Yafelman. That went on for some time. Afterwards, he had them return via the road along the sea. They rediscovered fish which, in their disaggregation, they had forgotten. If they couldn't find any along the coast now burning under the sun, they should go on out to dislodge them from the depths of the ocean. There were ships there, and sails, oars, and nets. The Watchmen stayed on the look-out behind the rocks, armed with slings.

For each son of the Earth still spared from the black fever, he made four workers: a fisherman, a hunter, a warrior, and a farmer, who dug into the hard earth in search of a bit of moisture, and spent hours attached to the waterwheel, drawing the last drops from the well. Everything from their labors was to be used in common. That lasted a long time: some of them rebelled against the new law, and Azwaw literally broke their backs.

Every day as he went to his house on the promontory, he counted up in his head the number of dead: those who died a natural death, and those who died under his own hand. Just so many bad branches pruned from the tree of the tribe.

"How many today, my little moon?"

"Eleven, Pa," replied Yerma, perched on his shoulders.

"That's all? Hmm. I thought there were more. My knuckles hurt."

Yes, decidedly, fewer were dying as the weeks went by, but why? Whole families remained in danger, and he had thought that if only he and Yerma survived in the long run, well, the two of them could engender a new tribe. Of that he was sure. It would take time, but he had plenty of time.

"Not too tired, my little moon?" he asked his daughter as he helped her to get down to the ground.

"No, Pa."

"Then come along."

And off they went to drink of the cold and abundant water. Generations of rains had gathered in an immense underground cistern. Far'oun the one-eye was not so crazy after all. His single eye had seen well into time. All one needed was to know what flagstone to lift up among the flagstones on the patio. But why let his brothers in on it? A little famine and **drought** had made them strangers one from the other—let them search for their own water and their own life!

"Come stretch out," said Yerma in her imperiously gentle voice. "Come rest beside me."

For some time now, Dada had been sleeping in the ass' lean-to far from the house, so that she wouldn't hear what she hates and loves at one and the same time—what she never moaned or cried out about. Life had broken her, but she didn't want to die. Not before Azwaw.

When he first saw Dada stretched out on her cot, the donkey said nothing. He went off by himself, not knowing where, but away from the lean-to. Consider the food that he gleaned from offal, the thirst that tortured him, the spur that dug into his emaciated rump, and the stinking cart-loads he pulled all day long. Such was his lot as a beast. He was patient, whatever the ordeal. Life is life, but he could no longer put up with the snoring of that two-legged old woman.

If Azwaw had rested one whole night or the space of a dream in the course of his lengthy struggle against the cowardice of his blood-brothers and against the elements and the unknown forces that represented the black fever, he couldn't remember it; his muscles and senses had been stretched taut constantly for such a long time. There had not only been the human beings. The gods had returned, more jealous and vengeful than ever, as terrifying as they were terrified. And a new God had emerged from the desert whose name was Allah and who drove everything before Him at a great pace. The drought, the famine, the sickness, and the fear of dying had created other priests, each with his own sphere of influence and his band of followers, as thin and surly as hungry hounds. Prophets increased in number and multiplied in imprecations, rending the slow, patient labor of forced cohesion and breaking down the community that had been about to be born anew into a multiplicity of clans.

"The Arabs are on the march. I can see them in my mind."

"Their God came down from the sun in a ball of flame. That is why everything in the world is aflame, I'm telling you!"

"They have broken through the mountain ranges, mounted on glittering dragons."

Meanwhile, the news of the latest battles came through from the North. The Rifains, the Aït Cherarda, and the Aït Snassen, valiant warriors if there ever were any, calling their brothers to come to their aid.

"Help! Arms, supplies, men!"

Covered with dust up to their hairlines, hardened by fatigue, emissaries followed emissaries. "Help!" But where were the supplies and the men? Like hurricanes, Azwaw and his Watchmen incessantly fell upon the preachers who had nothing but words in place of life over their groups of faithful, who had become nothing more than the ear of a jaundiced liver. Just thinking what the earth of the Aït Yafelman had been and what it could become again if only it had its sons back again (a luxurious paradise bathed by Mother Spring), Azwaw became like a crazy man, wilder than a beast. Was it so difficult, even impossible, to kill death?

That was when he was attacked. Priests from the ancient shadows and prophets of a hellish future had spread the word. Azwaw was the ally of the horsemen of Allah! He had sent them his best captains, who decimated other tribes and dried up the sources of the Oum-er-Bia, or at least deflected the river's course. He had betrayed the ancestral gods to serve their divinity without face or name. He deserved death. An ambush at nightfall. A dozen men armed with lances and truncheons. A detour on the steep path that led to the house on the promontory. Six men in front. Six men behind. Murder in their eyes.

Azwaw's senses had been sharpened for such a long time that he could detect the presence of someone holding his breath in the darkest night, all the more so when a stone had just come loose and rolled on the pathway. Before the stone could run its course, he had stopped and, in one single movement, put Yerma into a crag of rock ("Don't move! Don't be afraid!"), stretched out his arms, and turned around with a great prolonged cry to the Watchmen: "Yeeeeeeeeeeeehooooo!" The terrible balls of iron at the ends of the strings swirled frenetically, snapping wrists and crushing skulls.

"Don't kill them! Capture them alive! I want them alive! . . . ."

Of the eight or nine survivors, he made two lots, quickly sizing up the situation. He did not hesitate the space of a breath. He had the ones who were repentant chained to the pilings that supported the pontoon of the port. At low tide. During this period of equinox, the sea rose fast and high. As for the others, the worst ones, he named them forthwith district chiefs, and had his decision approved by what Elders were still alive. That was what had to be done. The portion of authority that they had just been granted would be exercised fully to subdue their brothers, given the fact that they had expected a death without mercy. Azwaw was certain of this. He smiled. Between them and him, there had been a pact, the outcome of negotiations carried out high-handedly and founded, at least insofar as it concerned him, on a will of refusal. However the case may be, he had acted in that way: to get what he is after, the negotiator should never leave the least doubt about his own capacity to break off negotiations.

7

It is in the house built on the promontory, as separate and solitary as a sentinel, that the three Councils now meet in plenary session. The house is solid and vast, dominating town, men, and events. It was there one night that Azwaw had perceived a gentle splashing that did not seem like any normal sound of the sea. He quickly ordered drums to be beaten and the fires of joy to be set: the river had returned. It was still thin and pitifully diminished, hardly trickling, as if it had just traversed a desert of great dimensions both in space and time, and now had found its bed once again. Whether standing upright in the riverbed or lying down, seated or dancing, the Aït Yafelman drank of its water, purifying body and soul, and sang and sobbed and laughed as though demented. The Oum-er-Bia was not dead! It was there once more! . . . .

> Athirsting, who will quench our thirst,
> if not you, our Mother Spring?
> Fallen on life's pathway,
> who will lift us to our feet
> and instruct us in the ways of truth, if you do not do so, eternal
> assif?
> Glory, glory, glory be to thee!

For whole days and nights, whether by the light of the moon or of torches, under rains that burst from the open skies in blessed downpours, through lightning, wind, and thunder, they stayed on the banks of the river, moving back only as the waters mounted. Grass grew again under their feet, trees around them became green, and the springs in the hills gushed forth once more like hymns to life. Gratitude throbbed to bursting in the people's hearts. Happiest of all were the priests and prophets, and the most peremptory in words—at least those whose legs had been swifter than the blows of Azwaw and the Watchmen. With their hands outstretched and their eyes afire, they went from one group to another: hadn't they announced it? Hadn't they explained the omens in clear terms?

"What am I going to do with them?" Azwaw asks himself, standing alone in the multitude that embraces his feet and hands and honors him like the greatest of gods, accompanying him everywhere to the sound of *bendirs* and sharp reed flutes. "What am I going to do with them all, each one of them, from the child suckling its mother to the old man hanging on my neck?"

No, he is not sad, in truth neither sad nor tired. He is more lucid than ever, perhaps even tender, now that the ordeal is over. Is it possible to leave one's native land one day, renouncing it with a turn of the back and then... and then to return as though nothing had happened in one's absence, as though there had been no need of you? The people who fled at the first sign of calamity are back again, kissing the nourishing Mother with full lips, the Mother they had abandoned to look after their own affairs. They are crying with love renewed, but the birds are also back once more, with legions of wings and cries, thrushes and sheep-vultures, rose-colored flamingos and ravens with yellow beaks, white ibises, bullfinches, nighthawks, and birds of paradise: this is their earth, their water, their peace. Who knows? They may have rediscovered the nest of their childhood where eggs are already incubating. Yes, even death creates life. That is what Azwaw says to himself as he listens by the ocean to their trills and cries, and the lowing of horned beasts down in the fat prairies on the hillsides, beasts that give birth to little ones.

If he has forgotten nothing, not a single word or gesture of cowardice, it is because he now knows that the future lasts as long as the past, both are created from shadow and light, and that is the significance of the alternating of day and night. When the horsemen of Allah arrive at the gates of this paradise that has just triumphed over all nights, all droughts, and even the dryness of heart most of its sons, yes, who will they find here before them? What faith? Deep inside Azwaw's head, an idea germinates. It is still unformed and vague, nothing more than the seedling of an idea—but it is already proceeding and stretching the length of all the centuries to come. He tries to give it substance, while he clasps Yerma to him with all his steely desire, causing her to cry out with life and death and resurrection as he spills his man's semen into her young body. whose form is both slender and full. Of course, the Councils can wait their time until the future of the entire community takes form in his skull. He knows that the Elders have had great difficulty in climbing the steep slope to his house because he had seen them with his own eyes, but they know the value of patience, being as old as they are. They can wait another hour or two, the time he needs to savor his pleasure to the fullest. Yerma is so fresh and full of ardor at daybreak. Every morning is rebirth.

The other one can also wait on her bed. Whatever happens, there will still be enough seed for her, for him. She came back with the river. He accepted her. On the other side of the bedroom door, on the patio, the members of the Council, biding their time as patiently as they can, whose discussions keep Azwaw from thinking clearly, only have need of words.

The rolling of drums, deep, heavy, and slow, is heard the length of the corridor. Its resonance tears like a lengthy fissure the sudden sounding of a reed flute at the entry to the patio open to the sky. Then all is silent. The silence of the drums melds with the silence of the men who have risen to their feet.

Under the intersecting lances of the Watchmen dressed in leather, standing rigidly at attention, Azwaw walks with measured steps, as though he has all eternity ahead of him— a graying man, thick-set, round-faced, mature, and smiling. His eyes are observant and comprehending, with a suggestion of laughter. Yerma follows him at a distance. She is a head taller than he. She moves with nonchalant steps and slack gestures. The coughing and whispering stops until Azwaw has seated his daughter on the coffer of honor, a chest that is covered with skins and lined with cushions, in the shade of a fig tree. He stays on his feet and smiles broadly. He says:

"Moushi, leader of the Jewish tribe, your herb medicines and your sorcery have vanquished the black fever. Your prayers have brought the river and all the rest back to life. May thanks be given to your ancestors and to your two gods. What are they called again?"

Moushi bows his albino head. With a gentle index finger, Azwaw lifts his chin. His voice is serious when he adds:

"These two metal balls that you gave to me one day in exchange for protection of your tribe saved my life."

Without expecting any answers, he turns on his heels and speaks to Hiempsal, the head of the Elders. Oumawch the bard has left this life, among the first to die. Happy are the blind of this world! Azwaw says:

"Hiempsal, the elder of our Elders, homage to your wisdom! It is you who showed me the ways of tenacity, even when my knees were trembling and my teeth were chattering from fear!"

He turns back his lips like a fox and bares his teeth to his very molars to Hiempsal. Then he says:

"I have only applied what you read in your calf's shoulder blade. It predicted that we would have to submit to the anger of the gods. Do you still have that old bone?"

Without turning around, he strokes the air like a swimmer with an oar, as he tries to quiet the tide of laughter that bursts against the walls of the patio. He says:

"And what does your shoulder blade have to tell about the men who fled their country? What should we do with them? We're listening to you. Go on, Hiempsal, read! Read in that ruminant's shoulder blade of yours!"

The old man turns the triangle of bleached bone, almost as petrified as he is himself, over and over in his hands. He lifts it up to the level of his eyes and interrogates it, not about the runaways but about himself; not about their near future or a later one, but about the immediate present. His lips move in silence, and Azwaw is filled with solicitude. He bends his head to one side, with one ear cocked. He says:

"Hiempsal has said that the law of laws commands that one brother must never abandon the other, nor the son his mother, no matter what the circumstances. Yes? You want to add something? Please speak up a bit more. I can't understand you."

Once more he leans over toward Hiempsal, who now only shakes his head forcefully. He appears to be listening to words, not one of which is uttered by a mouth smiling in fear. He turns to those present and says:

"Hiempsal, the eldest of the Elders, has just said that we must apply the law of exclusion. You all heard him as well as I, didn't you?"

And everyone, or almost everyone, approved. Yes, they heard very well.

"Exclusion from the community," continues Azwaw in a quiet voice. "That means, as you well know, that not a single hand touches the hand of those people, that not a single eye looks to them, and that not a single word is addressed to them. Oh, they are free to come and go as they wish, but the law of exclusion says that not a thumb's width of our soil should be tread by their feet and that not a door should be open to them. I do not speak of the heart. I think all of you have one. They should be as closed as mine is."

He takes the old man in his arms and kisses him on his left shoulder.

"I'm right in saying that that's what you told me to do before you said anything, aren't I? While you were peacefully sleeping away, you told me to apply the sentence, did you not? My Watchmen and I obeyed you this very night, and, consequently, we are now exclusively among Sons of the Earth. If you and I are both here standing in front of the Councils, it is to give account of your decision and mine in carrying out your orders as quickly as possible. Pick up your shoulder blade. One day you may need it to see the walkway in front of your steps, when no other community appeals to your light from the shadows. Go on, pick up your old rubbish!"

One man of highest rank has been waiting his turn for some time. He is not afraid. The words come tumbling out of his mouth so that he can hardly hold them back. In all the memory of the Berbers, such a thing has never been seen before, to have a leader as leader without having observed the proper forms. If only for the sake of formality, there is a discussion beforehand. Even if every single person recognizes the qualities of Azwaw, every one also expects to be consulted either by word or by glance. The elders are not to be treated lightly in these matters. They . . . . Azwaw goes toward him and quiets him with a slow movement of his hand. He says:

"Wait a moment, friend Mathô! Wait! Your words will have their place in a moment. From what I can see, you have not lost your divining rods in the tempest. Throw them into the air so that we may learn what they say of our destiny. Go on! Show us your science of the future."

Mathô's head is shaved from the nape to the chin, including eyelashes. Only in the middle of the skull is there a lock of white hair that has been rolled into a knot. Into that have been thrust three reed wands, of equal length, about that of the distance from a man's wrist to his elbow.

"What are you waiting for, Brother Mathò? You handled the little children at every turn to teach them the secrets of their days. I remember: I was one of them. Now that I'm an aging adult, and the Arabs are at the gates of our lives, I have more need than ever to know the destiny of our tribe—and perhaps to dream. Tell all of us present here what that destiny is to be. In a loud voice! And I who am your spokesman, I will try to carry it out if it is good; to turn it away, if it is against us. You're not afraid of the three pieces of reed, are you?"

"I am not afraid," says Mathò.

"Neither am I," concludes Azwaw. "Come closer, all of you! Come closer."

All of a sudden the wands fly into the air, then fall to the earth. Heads bend over them.

"What do they say," asks Azwaw.

"Two are almost parallel to the groove in this flagstone. You see that?"

"Yes, I see. So?"

"The third one cuts across them."

"It cuts across them. So?"

"Destiny has spoken."

"I did not hear it. Explain."

"It signifies that a danger is threatening us. That is very clear from the respective positions of the wands."

"Aha! A danger threatens us? First news! And what are we to do after that, according to you? What is the path to take to avoid this danger, if not to overcome it?"

Mathò questions the eyes of Azwaw, then picks up the wands, studying them a bit longer. Then he tosses them once more.

"And what do they say now?"

"Ah! Ah-ah! The first one goes from here to there, toward the east; the second is in a contrary sense, about two feet away; the last one fell a bit farther on. It is clear."

"What is clear?"

"The people of the Imazighen are going to be dispersed."

"It already is, from the darkness of time. One tribe is here, another there, others, who knows where. And within each one of them, they are divided into clans. But that is their business; it's none of mine. Let the brothers work it out among themselves. What I want to know is what we, the Aït Yafelman, have to do. What direction do we take? Do you suppose your tongue could wag a bit more and advise us?"

"Ah," says Mathò. "Ah-ah! . . . . We should . . . yes, we should think very seriously about the question . . . and then think about it and think about it . . . a long time, a very long time . . . ."

"And why not right away? We're here for that, aren't we?"

"We should consult the wand once more. They are the ones that know, but you need time and wisdom to comprehend, son."

"Aha! Time and wisdom! That means that if you toss them to the very end of the night and each time they fall in a different way, you would have your tongue to add destiny to destiny and prunings of words to words? Yes, Dada? I did not hear what you just said."

Quietly he walks over to Dada, and stops several inches from her, almost touching her.

"Yes, Dada?"

She spits in his face. He kills her, striking her with the edge of his palm across the throat. In the scuffle that suddenly hems him in, he says, without raising his voice:

"Her tomb is ready. Carry her away. It's going to get hot today."

Two Watchmen come up, take the corpse by the shoulders and the feet, and leave with their burden. The noise of their heavy footsteps fades away. The tumult ebbs. Azwaw has not stopped looking at Mathò, steadily. He says:

"Pick up your wands. Someone might step on them and break them, and then nobody would know our destiny. Not even you. Go on, pick them up! Bend that old back of yours and get down on your knees!"

His eyes make a sweep of the assembly, and he picks out this or that member.

"You, you, and you! You first, Suleika, the grandmother of the Jewish tribe. But you should not be trembling that way. Cast fear from your thoughts and look at me. Listen to me: your people live on the same lands as ours. You are a member of both the Council of Elders and the Council of Women. And then, you are of a different people from ours. Your cooperation is therefore precious above all. Search your memory. From what I know, it is the old women of the tribe to whom the stories of olden times were confided, as in a storage place, before your ancestors set out along the pathways of this world. Also, from what I was told, the Arabs are cousins of yours, right? Tell me."

"Well, Master . . ."

"I am not your master," he shouts. "Do you understand? I am the master of nothing and no one except myself. But I am not the only one! I am several. I am all of you, all of the community. And I need to know right away who these Arabs are, before they are really our masters. We have had to struggle against the calamities of the heavens and of the earth, and so time has escaped us. We must recover it, before another calamity befalls us. Is it true or isn't it true that these invaders are cousins of yours?"

"A little bit," answers Suleika. "A little bit, from olden times. My grandmother, who lived to be over a hundred . . ."

"Did she die? Well, so she's dead! What did she say, that woman?"

"She said that there were two cousins of the same blood at the same time, Isaac and Ishmael. Ishmael, that's them. Isaac, that's us."

"And so? Here also there are cousins. We are all cousins, more or less, but that does not enlighten me about Ishmael and his descendants. You, I know. I know your tribe. I know how to ally myself to you or to crush you, if need be. But I know nothing about the Arabs. Start from the beginning.

Tell me the differences between them and you. They are warriors, aren't they?"

"Our ancestors were warriors too. We have a book that relates their exploits."

"But you," says Azwaw, "you, here and now, you are no longer warriors in any way. You have become as quiet and as sad as chickens in the farmyard, pecking away at your past."

"It is our past!" protests Moushi in his corner. He is without fear or challenge.

"It's yours, of course! If tomorrow is behind you, behind your back, that's your problem, isn't it? For me, tomorrow is not something to wait for, but something to invent. You spend the greater part of your time evoking your past, with your lugubrious prayers . . ."

"They are our prayers!" says Moushi.

". . . like dogs howling at death . . . . And when you aren't praying, you are busy making cloth that our women wear instead of skins, and strange devices in yellow metal that they put on around their wrists and even in their ears with a little hole in them! And from the flowers you extract a liquid that they spread over their bodies as if their own odor were not sufficiently good for a man's nose! I can't put you in the front lines against your cousins because your hands don't know how to kill. You'd end up as the slaves of their women—go on, grandmother, tell us about the lands of the Arabs. It's to the east, isn't it? Near the lands of your ancestors, no?"

Suleika takes a deep breath and says:

"It used to be the same, for them and for us, at the beginning of the world. It is the land of Adam. It's there that he is buried."

"That was your first leader?"

"Adam is the father of man, and Houwwa is the mother of man. We lived there, those of us of the tribe of the Hebrews, near Yatreb, at Yaman. It is the land of our first guide, Abraham. Some of our brothers are still there at this hour we are talking."

"And so, why did you leave there? You had to submit to the law of exclusion, didn't you?"

The eyes of the old woman suddenly coil up like a snake, like those of a tiny child about to go asleep. She undoes her black fichu and lets it fall to the ground. Then she undoes the belt of her dress and lets it fall to her feet. Next she undoes her hair that she shakes like a sheaf of thongs, to the right and the left, faster and faster. Her voice takes on proportions of tremendous nostalgia as she begins again:

"The Eternal One sounded His voice one day, and we became His people among the peoples of the earth. He made a pact with us, and it is thus that He chose us, so that we would carry out His commandments. And then . . ."

"Don't shout like that!" screams Azwaw. "I'm not deaf!"

"Let her speak as she will," says Moushi. "It is our history."

". . . and then, He led us as far as the lands of the Philistines and the

Arameans. Praise be to Him, the Eternal One! It was the land that He had promised us, Eden, with orchards and gardens as far as one could see. And an immense river, the Jordan. Yes, our fathers obeyed the divine laws. When the time of disobedience came, a curse fell upon our people."

"Wait!" says Azwaw with extreme slowness. "Wait with your patience."

He bluntly shakes her and says:

"Wake up, grandmother. Set your eyes back in their place. Right now! You say there is a river there where your leader took you?"

"Yes, the sacred river. It is the Eternal One who . . ."

"Leave your eyes where they are. Look at me between the lashes. In the lands that you left for a reason I still don't know, did you also have rivers? No, don't close your eyes. No. Don't start letting your mind wander so as to put me to sleep too. I'm a Berber. Tell the Berber the truth true as a stone. Are there rivers in the lands of your cousins the Arabs?"

"No," says Soulika. "Only a few little streams, according to our history."

"Not a single river," adds Moushi, like an echo.

"Pick up the belt and scarf that you wear on your head," concludes Azwaw. "Give me your hand, little mother. Come rest a bit. Come along now."

He leads her over to the fig tree and gently seats her on the coffer beside Yerma.

"Relax now. You have told me the essential things."

He stays there, immobile, for an instant looking at his daughter—and, through her, at all the descendants of his descendants throughout the centuries. Then, without speaking particularly to her, as if not conscious either of himself or the others, he says:

"The Water."

He takes a few steps, stops in front of the Elder, and whispers:

"Mother Spring."

After that, he walks on and stops in front of a man of the Third Council. Then he tots up the names of the rivers of his land, one after the other, in a detached fashion, as if he were counting by cubic measure:

"The Bou Reg Reg . . . the Draa . . . the Sebou . . . the Moulaya . . . the Tensift . . . the Noun . . . the Beth . . . so many, many waterways!"

He turns toward Moushi, the rabbi, and asks him with a sort of quiet desperation:

"Do you know that water is the source of life? Has anyone told you, as my emissaries have pointed out to me, that the Arabs are now where there are the greatest rivers, the Nile, the Euphrates, the Tigris, and a number of others? And that where there is water, there is also time? Do you understand what that means? Are you and your brothers happy with my brothers and me ever since we welcomed you to these lands of ours that have also become yours?"

"Master . . ."

"I have already said that there is no master here! And we don't want any. Ever. In no way whatsoever. Moushi, leader of the Yahouds, adjust the words the length of your tongue before you answer this question: do you have a plan to save the tribe? Do you still want to drink your share of the water of Mother Spring?"

Moushi joins his hands in an intense moment of hope. He says:

"If the Eternal One has dispersed us throughout the earth, the Eternal One has . . ."

"Let's leave the Eternal One in peace! Do you have a human plan?"

"N-no. To tell the truth, no. All we do is wait and have patience. It seems to me that our brothers who live in other countries don't suffer too much by living with the Arabs, Praise be to the Eternal One! That is what some brother merchants who travel in caravans have told me. Our ancestors have lived side by side with the ancestors of our cousins."

"That is the past, and you have not lived through that experience. These things you are talking about are territories where you are not now living. And so, you know nothing but stories. Just consider one thing: time. Are you sure that your tribe will continue to live, in time? Do you have a plan for life?"

"No. To be truthful, no."

"Do you still have confidence in me?"

"We have always had confidence in you."

"Then go over to the coffer and sit down," says Azwaw. "Listen and wait. I had a little idea this morning. I'm just trying to verify it as I talk with this one and that."

He looks around the assembled group and turns to a sad, dry-looking man.

"It's your turn, Boucchous! I have sent you to the land of Hannibal. Mother Spring then was what she is now again. You did not see her without water. Tell us what you found out."

"Azwaw, there is no more land of Hannibal. It is the land of Kairouan that has replaced it."

"And the rivers?"

"And the rivers, and gardens and gardens, and between the gardens, houses the like of which you have never seen, even in your dreams. Nor have I."

"Aha!" says Azwaw. "What has happened to the Berbers? Are they still fighting to protect their water?"

"No, I have not seen them with arms in hand, or if they have any, it is at the gates to palaces. Perhaps they do! They are still fighting, but inside their houses, inside their hearts, at night when they are asleep. Or perhaps I didn't recognize them. The Arabs have been in those lands for a long time, after all. Do you want me to tell you, Azwaw?"

"Speak. Speak without falsehood, without flinching or padding."

"There are no more Berbers or Arabs."

"What do you mean?"

"There are only Muslims," says Boucchous.

He stands there first on one foot and then on the other, suddenly no longer sad, and then he declares:

"*Bismillahi rahmani rahim!* That means: "In the name of God, the Compassionate, the Merciful!' That is the password they all use. It's their way of saying hello, goodbye, and of shaking hands. They pronounce the phrase in a single breath before they sit down, before they go through any door, and even before they eat. *Bismillahi rahmani rahim!*"

So you learned the language of the conquerors, did you?"

"A little bit, in spite of myself. I have ears and a memory."

"But that is a fine thing, Boucchous! You can teach me that in case I have need of it. That could come in handy. You never know."

"Do you want me to tell you more?"

Azwaw looks at him very attentively and then says:

"Tell me the very last word of it."

"Listen to me, Azwaw! Listen to me carefully. In the countries over there, there is . . . there is peace. That is what I heard, saw, and felt. Peace between earth and man. That is what it is like in the country of Kairouan."

The silence that follows lasts a long time. Azwaw takes quite a while to break it. *Now he knows the time has come.* He is certain of his plan. He can communicate it to the three Councils, but he must prepare them for what he is about to say. They need words and smoke. He speaks with a luminous smile:

"And you came back to us?"

"Yes, Azwaw. I came back."

"Why?"

Boucchous looks at his hands, his feet, and the set faces that study him and come up to him. Azwaw's eyes are hot. With his hands stretched out, palms up and open as proof of his good will, he says:

"I don't know why."

"And it's because you don't know why that you are sad, my brother?"

Boucchous lowers his head and contemplates the future and the past that mingle with the length of his shadow on the ground, longer and more full of life than his body. He responds with confusion:

"Am I sad? Do I seem sad to you?"

"Go sit under the fig tree," says Azwaw. "On the ground, over there where there isn't any shadow. The sun will relax you from your trip and will disperse your dreams, perhaps . . . . Your turn next, Raho! You are not a dreamer, are you?"

Raho walks toward the center of the patio. He is small and beardless, about thirty years old. His laughter accompanied him from his very first step and has the whole assembly shaking with it.

"You are a warrior, a monkey's son of cunning and patience, right?"

"As for the warrior," answers Raho in a voice broken by hiccups and squeaks, "it could well be. As for the monkey, ha! . . . some times . . . heehee! . . . some times, if you're not one, heehee hoohooha! . . . War is sad for monkeys, ha!"

"Tell the councils what you told me, just the essential parts that they need to know. Do it in a few words, rapidly, so you can laugh to your heart's content down to the bare roots of your teeth."

"All right, you!" answers Raho, his face suddenly as long as a funeral.

He cracks the joints of his fingers as he raises three of them and says:

"The thumb, the index, and the other thumb. Azwaw sent me to the combat zones. He gave me three missions."

He folds the index finger:

"A well deserved success."

Then he folds both thumbs:

"Two defeats. Nothing more to say. That's all."

And he starts to walk away.

"One little moment," says Azwaw. "The brothers have not understood what you meant. They want some explanations."

"I should explain it to them? Really?"

"You certainly should. Explanations without explanations. You know the procedure."

"Right, Azwaw! So I took some fifty singed-heads with me. Azwaw assigned them grave responsibilities: to defend us, and to give a hand to the tribes fighting against the Arabs, the Aït Snassen, the Aït Cherarda, the Rifains, there to the north and the mountains. He named all of them military chiefs, that band of loud mouths and riff-raff. You know how magnanimous and generous he is . . ."

"I said no details."

"And so, no details to protect your modesty. In sum: these brave young men killed quite a few of the enemy, you should have seen how many! Then they were killed in their turn, dying valiantly in combat. The village now is rid of them. A great success, no?"

A threatening voice speaks out:

"And you, you're still alive?"

"I should think so," answers Raho mockingly. "I had two more missions to carry out."

"Go on with the story."

Raho scratches his ear, his nose, and the top of his head. Where should he begin? He says:

"Two defeats. Even though they were two good ideas. The first, according to Azwaw's instructions, was to try, as best as I could, to replace the older men with younger ones as the heads of the tribes, using every means possible in the human heart: jealousy, flattery, women, envy, the desire for power, and I don't know what else. I did everything I could to set one against the other and to excite the younger ones to try for their place in life. With few exceptions, the caciques did not want to be knocked off their pedestals, even with ropes around their necks. They hang on so to their positions of power! That's it."

He rubs his hands as though he could not go on, but he repeats with the most total expression of desolation:

"That's it."

"We don't understand," protest several of the Elders.

"You will understand in a moment," Azwaw assures them. "Raho, tell them about your third mission."

"Must I?" asks Raho, surprised.

"You have to freshen their ideas."

"Good! All right. As you probably don't know, Allah's horsemen have crossed the great mountain range. They are in our lands and have us surrounded. Every month that goes by brings them closer to our territory. So Azwaw racked his brain and pulled out a little monkey's flea: what if the other tribes fought for us, in place of us? Me, just a simple man, I had to take them presents for their chiefs, including some virgins—and fine promises with my hand on my heart: half of our cattle, five or six of our next harvests, the fish from our river, without mentioning the trumpets I spoke about a little while ago. Azwaw is generous. Of course, the mules and asses were a part of the journey, as they hauled the wagons full of the arms that our valorous brothers needed."

"And then?" says Azwaw.

"Then nothing. They fight for themselves, or very nearly. You could say that I failed in my mission."

"Why did you fail? Tell the members of the Council that are present here what they cannot understand without words. Tell about the Arabs. Empty your eyes of what you saw."

"The Arabs had the same idea as you, well before you had it, and they put it to work on a grand scale, without gifts or effort. Every tribe that they conquer is brought in with them for new conquests, as equals, in the name of Islam. That is their religion."

"Are there several tribes?"

"No. They are a single tribe. The *Oumma* or community."

"Have they several gods?"

"No. They have only one god, who is all the more present because he is invisible."

"How many priests serve this god?"

"None, and everybody. Everyone is his own priest."

"Now tell us about the leaders of the Arabs. Our brothers of the Councils still do not understand. Add words to your words. Tell them how many leaders the Arabs have."

"Only one. Oqba. The General Oqba ibn Nafi."

"He's an old man, isn't he?"

"No, Azwaw. He's my age, and his officers are equally young."

"Raho, come here, closer, even closer. I have something to ask you: do you want to be an Arab?"

"Yes," answers Raho, without the shadow of hesitation.

"Why?"

"For the same reasons as you do."

"Sit down, my brother," says Azwaw. "Thank you. I am going to ask counsel from the Councils."

As a man, cold, methodical, pitiless, his thinking always followed by action, Azwaw speaks to the Elders and asks a simple question:

"How many of you are there?"

As their eyes hesitate to look into his, and their answer takes time in coming, he hammers out each syllable that he pronounces:

"How-ma-ny-wise-old-men-of-you-are-here?"

"Twelve," finally declares an elderly man in a toneless voice.

"And you?" asks Azwaw, turning suddenly toward the Second Council. "How many women?"

"Also twelve . . . no, we are only eleven."

"And you, the active members?"

"Twelve, chief."

"Very well," concludes Azwaw. "Consequently you are thirty-five Berbers, thirty-five Aït Yafelmans in full possession of all the facts of the situation that have just been explained to you. It's up to you to arrive at conclusions and to decide the fate of the tribe."

Then he slowly withdraws several steps and takes in the whole assembly with his look, waiting. He stands there with arms crossed, holding in his breath. Not a nerve twitches in his face. The Watchmen have stealthily moved into place to surround the assembly and seal it off. There is the sound of a cough, and there is a murmur that grows louder and comes from the meeting groups. In the middle of the voices that become stronger and stronger, Azwaw loudly claps his hands and says:

"After mature deliberations, the three Councils meeting in plenary session have made a unanimous decision, which is the following: ours is an open city. We will offer no armed resistance."

Before the least surprise could materialize, he is already at the gate to the patio which leads to the path. He opens the gate with full force. Then he cries out vehemently in his cast-iron voice:

"I want to save my people! And I want to save it because I love it! It has need of gods, of masters, of guides, and is weak at times, despite its strength. But I love it and I will save it. It needs to be shown the way, and I will show it. I have had it called together to the very last child, to the very last invalid. Listen to them as they climb up toward you!"

He goes up to the thirty-five men and women, from one to the other, and addresses each one separately in an intense supplication:

"Do you have any other solution to save our race? Can you give me sons, ten, fifteen sons, that none of my women were able to give me and who could stand in my place?"

Thirty-five times, he repeats the same words, with the same rage from heart and gut:

". . . another solution?—the ten, twelve, fifteen sons . . . to take my place?"

There is, of course, a hand that is raised, a word that is chanced, but he sweeps them aside immediately, and chases them off like little gadflies in the immensity of the time that he inhabits. "Quiet! Quiet all of you!" Then he says:

"You too, I love you, but at the same time, I hate you. And I hate you more than I love you because you have still not understood, you, the representatives of our tribe. Year after year, catastrophe after catastrophe has fallen on our city, and I have never ceased replacing the members of the Councils with two-footed animals with a bit more ardor. But you are all the same once you have control of a little power. That's enough to make you waste away. Among those of you who are present here, there are some of my own men, with all the vigor that is called youth. You have not understood what has happened to the other tribes. They rose up against the invaders, yes indeed! But afterwards they themselves were urged to insurrection by Islam. With the two holes in the sand that you call eyes, you have been unable to see clearly what has happened to our brother Boucchous. It was enough for me to send him to the land of Hannibal for him to come back cut in two, half Muslim, half Berber. The two rings of leather that are stuck at one and the other side of your heads have not heard what Raho explained very clearly to you: these Arabs are not the same kind as the conquerors who preceded them. They are searching for something they do not have in their own territory: water. And I have also told you that where there is water, there is also time."

All of a sudden Azwaw feels very tired and very much alone. From the bottom of what he sees in the future as from the depths of the past, he cries out:

"Our ancestors had to face the Roman invaders and many others who spent no more than a century or so on our soil, sometimes more and sometimes less, and they pillaged us, no doubt, and enslaved us, no doubt, but without reaching our soul. They did not destroy us because we are still here on our lands. They destroyed themselves. They did not know the value of time. Now, the Arabs, being sons of the desert, know that better than anyone else. The other conquerors were interested in the earth and the riches of the earth, and I assure you that these Arabs are interested first and foremost in man, in what he is, and in what he can bring to them. They intermingle with the Berbers, in their blood, to found one single same tribe, the *Oumma,* as they call it. The emissaries that I sent out here and there have brought me the proof of it. That is why I tell you that these new conquerors will remain here a very long time, if not forever. From East to West they are busy accomplishing what I have always hoped for: the increase of the race and the perpetuation of the blood. Moreover, they have for themselves what their predecessors lacked: not several gods, but one single god. And no priests. Raho told you a little while ago that this god is in every one of them. Do you know what that signifies? Every horseman of Allah is alone and never alone at one and the same time. He is the master of his life, and, at the same time, he feels that he is understood, loved, protected, and pushed ahead. That is their strength. Faced with that force, what do we have to oppose them with?"

"Our own force," shouts one thundering voice. "We must fight."

"Who said that?" asks Azwaw with a soft voice.

"I did."

"Come forward."

It is a man of the Third Council, as strong as a rock. He repeats obstinately:

"We must fight."

"How many of us were there before the drought, the famine, the sickness, and the death?" Azwaw asks him.

"Ten thousand. Ten or eleven thousand."

"How many are we now?"

"About half that."

"Is that counting the refugees?"

"Yes. That's with the refugees."

"That's all," concludes Azwaw. "You have said what you had to say. You can draw your tongue back into the protection of your teeth. Don't cut it on the way back in."

"We have to fight," shouts the other as loud as he can. "Fight! We're not going to let our throats be cut like . . ."

"Take my knife," says Azwaw quietly. "Go on. Don't be afraid. Take it! Now I have no weapon, and I never will have. Neither I nor my children nor the children that they will have in all the centuries to come will have weapons. No weapon, except time. You also, in addition to your knife, will have time at your disposal, and so will your descendants and the descendants of your descendants. But I and mine, we will always have *a little bit more time* than you and yours. Do you understand that? We will always have an advantage over you . . . . Wait a minute! Don't snort like an ox. Let me explain to you the stakes and the rules of our combat. With patience, if you have any. You are already in a hurry and, at that rate, you will be beaten before I've stopped talking with you. Wait a minute . . . . Let's look at the situation. Either you kill me or I take your life. If you die, your children will still be there. They will be faced by my children, plus me, plus all of our time to bring things to their end. It's a simple matter, isn't it? You say that they will be able to exterminate all of us? Impossible, absolutely impossible! You forget the extra time that is our advantage. During that extra time, one of my descendants will have procreated a new generation—and so on, endlessly. But you, you will come to an end, one day or another. Wait a minute, brother! Don't be so impatient . . . . Consider the other eventuality. You take my life. Fine. Then there will be only you and yours and mine, and even then, whatever you do, my descendants of future centuries will walk on the tombs of your final descendants, only because they had a cubit more of time than you. Now do you understand?"

"No," answers the man instantly. "Nothing. That's too complicated for me. I'm only a simple countryman."

"I'm going to explain to you in terms of a countryman. Let's suppose that you and I have a field, one single field for the two of us. You are good grass, flowers, vegetables, and cereals. Me, I am the weed, the crabgrass, the nettles, and the prickles that are useless, even for feeding the asses. The *sedras,* for example, if you know them."

"I know them."

"Our battle will consist of planting, you the good grass, and I the bad, in this field. We have plenty of time."

"I'll pull you up," says the other one with a big smile.

"Fine. You pull me up, but I'll pull you up too. It's easier to pull you up, the good grass. Crabgrass and *sedras* have roots all over, very deep, as you know. And every time one of us pulls up the other, it will occupy its terrain to plant again. Tell me, in the end, which will choke the other?"

"The bad grass, darn right!"

"So you finally got it," says Azwaw. "Give me back my knife. We won't need any weapons to vanquish the Arabs. We'll just be the bad grass that we are. Our city has been declared an open city since yesterday. We have been decimated by the catastrophes of earth and sky. I don't want war to reduce us to nothing. If there is a plan to save our tribe, other tribes will also know about it—and I will utilize it, you can be certain of that—it is the question of time. Listen to me!"

Who is surrounding him? Whose dozens of hands touch him? Who lifts him up on their shoulders so that everyone can see him? To what beings does he address himself? To those who have come up from the city and who have just invaded his house to bursting, even on top of the roof? Or to the Berbers who will one day be born and whom he carries inside himself, in his vision and in his great patience? Is he the only one who believes in his plan? If he knew that a single Aït Yafelman, woman, man, or child, shared his faith, he would not say a word. He says:

"They sing, the horsemen of Allah, as they gallop their horses. Nothing can resist them; nothing frightens them. They are happy, even when they die. Others, still more numerous, still more ardent, take their place. They are a single community. They have only one goal: the future. And one cannot struggle against the future unless our own future is clearly traced and defined once and for all, without deviations. This very day. Here it is: we are going to occupy time's terrain. We are going to get *inside* these new conquerors, inside their very soul, into their Islam, their customs, their language, into everything that they know how to do with their hands and to say with their hearts. Into everything that is youthful, strong, and beautiful. We will slowly sap their vigour and then their life. Very slowly. We have the time. We have all the time of eternity. They won't let themselves be taken in very easily, but we will reach our goal with our bad grass and prickly roots. The earth is reborn every spring-time, the river also, the Ocean. Why not us? We have lived for ourselves for ages and ages inside our own territory to the point where we have impoverished ourselves in ideas. We need to renew ourselves. What could be our death is going to give us new life. We will bend our backs, that much is certain. We will undergo vicissitudes without name, that much is

74 / Driss Chraibi

sure. We will do everything we can to pass by unnoticed, inoffensively, stupid and bewildered to Arab eyes. We will act as though we were transformed on contact with them. We will even be grateful to them. Nevertheless, our faith and our Berber heart will survive within us more full of life than ever. Patience, patience! We will maintain our customs, our language, and our traditions alive in our homes, for ourselves. As for me, I tell you: even when I am dead, I'll keep my obsession with water and my even greater obsession with the light of my country in my bones. Patience, patience! Time is with us. We will give the greatest of pleasures to our tomorrow's masters: we will be the most faithful of the faithful in their new religion. As for taking, if the latter can give us new sap and new slips for our tree, well, we will accept it as so many benedictions.

"The Arabs may be happy with us, once we become Muslims like them. They will let their guard down and will let us live and procreate. We will doubtlessly never be their equals. It is the law of domination that makes things go, masters and slaves. The slaves that we will become will hold the life of our earth and of our river forever locked in their memory. What can happen? They will appropriate our lands, that is for sure, but they may not bring death to it. Earth always regenerates after the death of men. The Oum-er-Bia, our sacred river, they can drink its water as much as they like, but even as many as they are, would they be capable of drying it up? An *assif* always comes to life again, you saw it with your very eyes, but we, the Sons of the Earth, if we do not find a way to win the battle of time, we lose our last drop of blood. On the contrary, we want to preserve our blood and to strengthen it with their blood. Our sons will join with their daughters, and our daughters, with their sons. Every child that is born will be a Berber in blood and heart for us, even if he carries the name of his father. That will be from generation to generation, with new branchings, ever more vast and more vigorous as time goes by. It will be subterranean as well, as every one of our descendants will go on procreating inside the descendants of the Arabs.

"It is a simple matter. We will have time from time. Nothing, neither misery nor opulence, will make us lose sight of what we are proposing: to survive them. And we will survive them. We will survive them because, with the certainty of fate, our blood will end up submerging theirs. As for our land, you all know it. You are its sons. It loves only its children. It is savage and beautiful, and very strong, stronger than all the invaders that wanted to dominate her in the past. She has been their cemetery. The Arabs will fatten it with their cadavers and the cadaver of Islam one day soon, in a few centuries. Their last descendants, if there are any, will only turn toward the past of their ancestors, and that day, we, the Imazighen, we will be the future."

He is not conscious of the heavy silence that his last words have brought, nor does he hear the tempest of ovations that arises all at once. Suddenly, without any preliminaries and without even looking at what he is doing, he pulls out his knife, pulls up his sleeve, and slashes his forearm with the point of the blade: a fish encircled by a star. He says:

"The sign of olden times. I do not want an oath of words. Words die long before the mouth has pronounced them and the faith that gave them birth. I want an oath of blood, as in other times when the first Aït Yafelmans pledged their allegiance to the Oum-er-Bia as they offered her a bit of their blood. Each one of you take a knife. Make the sign: a fish for the river, the star for its children. Go down toward your Mother Spring. She is waiting for you. Merge several drops of your blood with the eternal sap. Walk into the water up to your waist and say: 'I, a Berber of the tribe of the Aït Yafelmans, I pledge an oath to have the patience of patience, the tenacity of tenacity, and the endurance of all endurance!' "

He had left the house some time ago, and everybody had followed him or preceded him as he was carried in triumph from one arm to the other down to the bank of the river. In the midst of these fervors that surround him, he now knows that the future has really begun. The beginning of time. In the cries, in the sobs, he feels the alleviation of the Sons of the Earth, who are finally alleviated from themselves and their past. He has just given them a destiny, a goal to be attained—a distant one, no doubt, but a goal. Why was it necessary to get to the edge of extinction for them to stand up to life? What will happen to them when he, Azwaw, is no longer there to whip them and push them to the fullest of their resources?

He is the first to plunge into the Oum-er-Bia. Splashing about, he kisses the surface of the water with both lips, and cries out:

"Repeat these words: 'I swear to preserve the memory of my people in all circumstances, no matter what.' "

"We swear it!"

"Repeat these words: 'I swear to transmit to my present and future descendants, the plan of our survival and to . . . and to make them swear to transmit it faithfully to their own descendants, wherever they may be or wherever they may live, from one generation to another, until the end of time."

"We swear it! We swear it, Azwaw! . . . Az-waw! . . . Az-waw . . .' "

"This river, this earth beyond these two banks will find their children once again one day. We will meet again in ten centuries, in fifteen centuries. That is a small matter in terms of time, isn't it?"

That morning of the year 679, Azwaw almost drowned in the sacred river. All the Aït Yafelmans had walked into it by turns. He had become their god.

SECOND TIDE

1

Dawn. Do you know what dawn is? And who will ever tell you what dawn is?

General Oqba ibn Nafi rode on horseback at the head of his troops, rode irresistably from the Gate of Africa, rode in the panting of steeds at a gallop, in the sparks flashing from their hoofs, in the clouds of dust that rose to the heavens, in the continuous surge of Islam in its dawn. The dawn of humanity was in him, in each of his acts, each of his words, Koranically. It was as if he were not of this century, but had been born dozens of years before, at the same time as a shepherd of the tribe of the Quraysh named Mohammed, and had received with him, in a grotto in the Arabian desert, the first revelation (*"Recite! Recite in the name of your Lord who created man from a drop of blood! Approach! Prostrate yourself! And listen!"*) and all of the revelations that later became the Book. Yes! Certainly yes! By the soul and He who brought it equilibrium, it was as if Oqba, along with the Prophet, had known the gigantic emotion and dazzling commotion of hearing the divine Word. He was fully convinced of having lived through the exile, the Hegira, all the combats of the first companions of the human community, and the whole fulfillment of its destiny, and then . . . and then this return stripped bare, sobbing, chanting in Mecca. When Bilal, the black *muezzin*, the first slave freed by the Prophet, had climbed to the top of the temple of the Ka'ba where the idols of darkness once had reigned, and with his immense voice, his immense faith, had cried out the first call to prayer, it was as though he, Oqba ibn Nafi, had climbed up there that day with him, in him, and had shouted the words peace, PEACE, the reconciliation of men with themselves, with all the kingdoms of Creation, to the four corners of the horizon, to the two Orients, the two Occidents, to the two seas, and to all the suns of the universe.

It was on the *djebel* Rahma, the Mount of Mercy. The Prophet had united his people there at the end of his life. He had asked them three times this question full of triumph, serenity, and doubt: "In the name of God, the master of the worlds, have I accomplished my mission?" A few days later, he left this life. How the mourners wept and continued to weep for their departed loved one!

But, Allah akbar, his work was living and made him more alive than ever, bringing new birth! *Wa shamsi wa douhaha!* as the Koran says, "by the sun and its rays," Islam was dazzling! More full of light than the sky illuminated by the constellations, it triumphed over night, magnificently celebrated as time extended over the earth. There in the lands of the east, General Khaled ibn Waled had carried it like a blinding torch to the very sources of the Tigris and Euphrates. And to the south, the horsemen of Allah, streaming through the waves, had crossed the isthmus of the Red Sea that separated the Orient from the Occident, and then had gone up the Nile, galloping toward the Sudan. Further on, beyond the steppes and mountains of Asia, other armies were on the march in the direction of the Ganges and the lands of the Hindus. Who could stop them, or what could, if not the end of the continent? Everywhere, in floods, men took up the new religion. Had the Book not so declared, in terms of life? "By those who are sent wave after wave to blow upon the tempest, by those who spread out and separate and proclaim the recall, that which is promised you will come! It will come when the stars shall be wiped away, when the heavens shall be rent, when the mountains shall be pulverized, when the hour shall be announced to the messengers. When will the due date come?" The due date had come and had exploded the long, long darkness in which people had lived. Each horseman, each horse, was a messenger from God, the carrier of the Message.

In pursuit of the sun in its place of rest came Oqba ibn Nafi, with ten thousand men and ten thousand horses. In the holster of each saddle, there was a handful of the natal earth of Islam. The horse was everything: the friend, the brother, the father and the mother, the son and the ancestors. It was the pupil of the eye. The horse was taken care of first, before and after any battle. Whether in bivouac or at a halt, it was by his side that men slept. He was the most beautiful of all Creation: short ears, just like the pasterns and the tail; neck, legs, hips, and stomach long; the forehead, breast, and hips, wide. Children of the desert, a mixture of fire and wind when the Bedouins mounted them, they were not ten thousand combatants on their mounts, but a single being, a single entity, living and vibrating from the hoofs to the human word.

The unbridled music of the hoofs' hammerings spread from earth to sky. Who had pretended that the Prophet was dead? And why weep? "*Do not adore me,*" he had said. "*Do not adore my corpse. I am only a man like you. Be intermediaries among the peoples. Be witnesses of the Divine Verity as I am a witness before you.*"

There were ten thousand witnesses under the command of General Oqba ibn Nafi. The train of equipment was followed by twenty thousand camels and forty thousand goatskins of water. In the vanguard, several days to the rear, came the carts carrying the greatest learned men of this century: doctors in law, professors, architects, builders, artists. Oqba was only opening up the way, cutting through the darkness.

He did not consider himself a warrior and had never wanted to be one. His war was one of faith. According to the dictum of the Koranic affirmation, "to kill a single human being is to kill all the human race": he brought death to no one unless he had previously sent forth an emissary and had made a personal visit with a small escort. A small man of fragile nature, wrapped in a brown woolen mantle, wearing leather sandals whose thongs were wrapped around his legs up to the knees, he stepped onto the earth. With his aquiline nose, thin and sparse beard, and hawk-like eyes, he would sit down and look at the chief of a tribe, a town or a country, the stranger who tomorrow would be either his brother or his enemy, and inevitably declare:

"Say: 'I bear witness that there is no divinity but Allah and that Mohammed is His prophet!' Say "God is unique. God is indivisible. He was not begotten and He has not engendered. He has no partner or equal.' "

He gave time for everybody to reflect and to meditate on these things, for them to descend into their souls. He waited a night. If despite all, their reply was negative, he asked them, under solemn pledges, to come under Islam's protection and pay tribute, in exchange for which they would be granted the right to continue as they were, with their own customs and laws. As for the earth, it belonged to everyone, which is to say God. It was to become once again what it had been in the beginning, the cradle of the human community, from one horizon to the other. It was only when their was total refusal without issue that Oqba engaged in battle. Before he did so, however, he read some verses of the Koran, asking for help and reciting his last daily prayer, to which he added the Prayer of the Dead, as much for the enemy as for himself and his soldiers:

> *Misery is our misery and perishable are our bodies!*
> *Allah akbar! There is strength only in Him!*
> *Recourse only in Him, life only in Him!*
> *And, when there shall be nothing left of the world,*
> *the Sublime Face of God will remain!*
> *Allah akbar! Allah akbar! Allah akbar! . . .*

"*Allah akbar!*" intoned the Bedouins of Oqba, standing in their stirrups.

They swallowed a pinch of their original soil as a kind of provision for their journey, and knotted veils around their heads at eye level. Nostrils distended and trembling at the sound of the ample funerary chant, their horses stamped and pawed the ground. They also knew the signal.

Oqba always attacked at dawn. Animals and people were fully prepared. And, in Arabia, the dawn came so early and the light so instantaneously, without shadow or horizon, so dazzling, that the sons of the desert learned to live with the rhythms of the sun from earliest infancy. His men were up as soon as he, and as fervent, while in other places awakening was as crushing as the pains of giving birth. The overpowering heat and the bitter night cold that sometimes brutally followed it, the torrid simoon, and the sand storms that suddenly arose and smothered everything in their path, all were their element. The nudity of life between an arid soil and a flaming sky was a force that could only sustain some ageless date palms rooted in the rock, and men ready for anything and horses of fire.

That very nudity corresponded perfectly with the nudity of Islam. It did away with time and overflowed its banks: "*Work for this world as if you were to live eternally, and for the world to come as if you were going to die tomorrow. . . . Divine Creation is continuous.*" It did away with all sense of anguish and guilt. Under the influence of Iblis, the accursed angel, Adam and Eve had indeed eaten of the tree of immortality in order to attain an imperishable reign, in God's place. But God had pardoned them—they had gone astray. He had chosen them from among all His creatures to represent Him on earth. Death itself was not considered an end, an annihilation, the unknown, but as a prolongation of life, a return to the Creator: "*We will gather together your bones wherever they may be, and We will cause you to be born again.*" There was no intermediary, no intercessor, no priest or idol or representation of any kind between God and man: "*My temple is the universe, and the heart of man is my altar.*" That had been said aloud in Arabic, in the Book that every combatant knew word for word from the first to the very last verse.

Mohammed was one of their own, an orphan born into very modest circumstances, whom God had elevated to a state of perfection. Their commander-in-chief was of the same tribe of the Quraysh as the Prophet. He had paid no attention to the entreaties of the Caliph Omar ibn al-Kattab, the Prince of Believers, who had declared three times to his generals:

"*Ifriqiyya al-moufarriqa!* North Africa disperses. It will disperse the Muslim community. I will never send anyone there as long as my eyes can still weep."

Omar was a mystic and a preacher. He took the Prophet as his example in action and word. On his death, he was succeeded by Othman, and then Mou'awiyya as head of the caliphate, but they had their eyes turned toward the Orient. He, Oqba ibn Nafi, looked to the land of the setting sun, where he foresaw that the future would arise. Behind the other horizon was the other half of the world about which almost nothing was known, except its barbarity. He had united his horsemen in a circle on the borders of Tripoli. Standing in the center of the circle, he had given the order for the following day, taking it from the Koran:

"'*It is God who reigns in the heavens and on the earth. it is He who ordains life or death. He is the first and the last, without beginning or end. He is apparent and hidden in all things. He knows who waters the earth and who leaves it, who descends from the sky and who ascends into it. He is with you wherever you may be!*' Forward! Forward in search of the sun!"

The army of Africa got under way. Cities and fortified places fell before him. Plains, valleys, mountains, and peoples slipped by. After each battle, Oqba asked the vanquished:

"Is there something beyond you?"

The reply was:

"Yes. Jarma, the capital of the Fezzan."

Once Fezzan was conquered, he asked:

"Is there something further on?"

"Yes. The fortresses of Kuwwar."

He seized the king of Kuwwar who was in his castle and whose troops had given him a hard time. He cut off his finger.

"That is a good lesson for you. You could have had a humane discussion with the representative of Islam that I am. When you look at your severed finger, you will no longer think about fighting against the Muslims. Is there anything beyond this kingdom?"

Without forewarning, he turned back at full speed and cut off the ear of a Berber chieftain:

"That will serve as a lesson to you. Every time you go to touch your ear, you will remember that it is not good to submit to Islam as you have done, and then to break your word as soon as I have turned my back. God abhors renegades. He knows what men have in their hands and what they hide behind their backs. The next time, I will cut out the tongue that made the pledge. For now, give a thousand *dinars* to each of my soldiers and two thousand *dinars* for their horses. Your money chests must be full given all the time that you have been selling olives from your fertile lands to the Europeans. I am only God's creature, but I have my look-out men and my spies. See to it that the other tribes hear about this, if you want to keep the other ear that is listening to me right now."

He used the tactics of a fox. He divided his army into three parts: one squadron under the orders of his lieutenant Bousr; two others confided to Charik; and the greater part of his forces remaining under his own command. Bousr charged for the attack, but then wheeled around and fled before an enemy that was superior in number. Midway, he reversed himself and charged again, joined by Charik's horsemen. During this time, Oqba had cut behind the adversary, suddenly falling on them from the rear and cutting off all possible escape. Sometimes he sent a detachment to stir up the dust, using special horses trained for display. Stirring up clouds of dust all around a city, neighing like creatures out of hell. Nothing but horses, day and night. The men rested in peace, a gallop's distance away. Thinking that they were being beseiged by a multitude of multitudes, the inhabitants opened up the gates to their city. Not a drop of blood shed.

"What lies beyond this city, in the name of God, the All-Powerful?"

Oqba payed no attention to certain strongholds. He went by them as if they did not exist, tranquilly continuing his march toward the far west. He would let time do its work. Isolated, like little islands in the interior of lands solidly conquered, these places could only break down and eventually succumb. An ironclad order had been given to the populations of the conquered lands to have no commerce with the rebels, neither in water nor bread. Not even in words. The new converts to the religion of God took the responsibility of zealously watching over the observance of the Law: "No, I shall not swear by that city! I am freed from that city. I shall not swear by its inhabitants, neither its fathers nor its mothers, nor those to whom they have given birth!" That was not a renunciation on their part. It was simply that they had just left their tribe to enter into a vaster, younger, and warmer community. Had Islam not been born in exile?

Oqba overturned idols and their servants as soon as he passed the gates of a city. His horse would rear up in the pagan temples, neighing and breaking with his hoofs everything that represented to the commander-in-chief the personification of death. He knew how easily death can dominate life, and he, Oqba, intended to bring about the triumph of Islam, which is to say, of life. He did not want to conquer anything in this world that was only appearance in the face of reality, not a thumb's breadth of land, not an ounce of gold, not even what people call glory. If a war was holy, he was certain that it was his war. Let the others drown in power and opulence, the caliph in his palace to the east, the king of Egypt who made and unmade generals! He would continue his battle throughout the night. One day the sun of Islam would rise in the west.

The army of educators and builders who followed him did the rest. They had all the time they needed to uproot the weeds and to sow God's grain in men and soil. The "dusty poor" were richly nourished according to the precepts of the Koran; the feeble were taken up, and orphans were given special care. Slaves were set free and captives were liberated. They took the place of the previous leadership. No master who had lived with power could have accepted with a light heart the need to return to his origins, to be a simple member of the community. Temples were destroyed and council buildings were razed, and in their place mosques were constructed, houses of God open to all. Crowds entered them in closed ranks, with bodies washed and shoes left at the gate, wearing no jewelry or ornament of any kind, all equal, not before chieftains or kings, but before the Master of Worlds. "Everywhere you turn, you encounter His face."

Water. "From water have We made all living things." At the entrance to each mosque, that was the first thing that met the eye and the ear: water spouting like the notes of a cithar into the basins for ablutions. The sky and light came from on high. On the ground were mats. The walls were blank, and, like witnesses of stone, the minarets rose up from where the muezzins cried out their call to prayer five times a day, to the four horizons, filling it with their capacity for belief and for love, exploding each word that they shouted to express their emotion, resounding from earth to the heavens:

Allahou akbarou Allahou akbar!
I bear witness that there is no divinity but God!

I bear witness that Mohammed is His prophet!
Take care for your prayer! Take care for your salvation!

Whether atop the mountains, or the plain, in the oases, at the sources as well as at the mouths of rivers, everywhere was the same voice, interchangeable and vibrant, uniting the new humanity from the Irak to the Atlas, in an uninterrupted suit of fervors, without space or time:

Allahou akbarou Allahou akbar!
Take care for your prayer! Take care for your salvation!

An ordinary man walked out of the sparse crowd. He went toward the wall of the mosque that was exposed to the east, where a niche was carved out. He had no book in his hands, be he a saint, nor did he have any man-made object with him, be he a priest. He had his everyday clothes on his back. Alone, very alone in front of the niche, he recited several verses that the wall reflected back to him and immediately, by the magic of his words and voice, he became the Prophet, in the grotto of Hejaz where once the Voice had resonated:

God is the light of the heavens and of the earth.
His light is like a niche with a lamp;
The lamp is in glass;
The glass is like a sparkling star;
The lamp is illuminated by a sacred tree,
An olive tree that is from neither Orient nor Occident,
And whose oil would give light without fire having touched it:
Light on light.
God guides whomever He wishes toward His light.
It is in houses where His name is invoked,
And where He is honored, morning and evening,
By men whom no commerce nor barter
Can distract from His memory . . . .
The man to whom God does not give light
Has no light . . . .

What he recited had no meaning in the words of the tribe, the words that they had known up to then, and with which they had been born. The Koranic words, more ancient and yet more modern, were revealed before the mother and after all death. Each one had its own music, no matter how one moved the tongue in one's mouth. And it was this music that was the first sense, the one that unbolted the prison of the brain and went on to descend into the sources of the emotions of the body.

As they left the mosque, people accosted each other, mutually transformed, as if they had just come to know themselves, overwhelmed in heart and appearance. Now there was a discovery that was stronger than any adherence to a common history or blood; no man of any people was alone. He was an integral part of the universe. Oqba knew what he was doing in building mosques before he constructed barracks or palaces, and in bringing the greatest doctors of the Law. His conquest was one of souls.

General Amrou ibn al-Ass, General Houdaij, and all those who had preceded Oqba at the head of the armies had only scraped the surface of North Africa. They wanted to conquer lands. Their war started and stopped with the point of their sword; their Islam did not go beyond the Arabic ethnic group. They laid siege to a fortress and entered it with spirit and bravery. After the fortress was sacked, the generals would send their army train back to the opulent Orient of central power (with slaves, booty, gold in bars, and gold in coins) as if they should receive their sanctions from their superiors and not from God Himself. They were then besieged in turn by the local people of the *bled*. King Gregory, whose lands extended from Tripoli to Tangier, had been killed in combat, but other Berber chieftains took his place: la Kahina and her murderous warriors, and the elusive Kousaïla Lamzam whose commandos seemed to shoot up out of the earth and whose chief target was the water supply. Every time that the Arabs dug a well, the combatants of the night filled it up just as quickly. They made all of the watering places disappear one after another. Islam and its sons had to be deprived of all water.

Newly appointed General Oqba had purged and restructured his army from top to bottom. He sent home the Egyptians and Syrians with their glory, their wounds, and their merits still fresh. He also sent home the Arabs from towns and from comfortable backgrounds, and kept with him only the Bedouins who had learned endurance and patience, who knew no thirst and who lived on dates and onions, and could remain immobile for days on end on watch, and then charge into combat at a moment's notice. Islam was their only country. Except for their horse, God, and their commander-in-chief, they knew no one and nothing, not even the rustiness of a nail or of a thought.

Yes, it was in Ramadan, the month of fasting, that they gave all their strength, as though they were drinking and eating the ascetic and the war, liberated from their very bodies. They were certain that they would enter Paradise in their saddles, fully equipped. When they fell in combat, other Bedouins of the reserve mounted their saddles which were still warm from their bodies; and when their horses died, chargers the color of blood and of flame sprang forth from the Orient.

There was a week's forced march in the direction of the city of Khawar. It was conquered at dawn. Oqba took possession of all its riches and distributed them among his warriors. He put all the inhabitants of fighting age to death, for they had killed the peaceful emissary whom he had sent in advance to ask for submission to Islam. He spared the children for the mosque, the schools where they would be taught the ins and outs of society through the Koran. The Koran was everything: language, grammar, syntax, poetry, law, jurisprudence, philosophy, music, and, above all, science. Three years for each child, and then came the study of the *hadiths*, the acts and words of the Prophet. The Arabs did not understand or want to understand anything but Arabic. From the Hedjaz, from Yemen, from the countries of the east, came the best sons of the new civilization as the decay of the Byzantine, Roman, and Berber kingdoms progressed.

Suddenly avoiding the roadway where the Berber commandos were waiting for him, Oqba went in a straight line toward Morocco, passing by the territory of the Mouzata, whose citadels he captured. He built mosques and schools. Waterways, colonised even before the land. Ghadamis taken by a single corps of cavalry. Gafsa conquered and eighty thousand prisoners taken. Qastilyya conquered, the fortress of fortresses of the Berbers, the Romans, and the Afariks. More mosques and schools. Small and upright on his horse, coughing and spitting blood, Oqba ibn Nafi cried out with each victory to his legion of educators:

"I confide these new-born of Islam to your care. You will answer to me with your head. End my war with the only war that is: peace. I shall return to inspect your work, if God grants me life."

Oqba carefully visited the city of Karouan that General Houdaïj had founded several years earlier and that was spoken of throughout the Arabic empire. He had it razed. At some distance from there, he ordered a valley planted with trees and vegetables, by a river, the *oued* Marguellil.

"Inhabitants of the valley," he cried with all his strength, "leave this place and may God have mercy on you! We are going to install ourselves here."

For three days, he proclaimed this invitation to leave, and had it announced by his heralds. He transformed his horsemen into woodcutters and diggers.

"Cut down those trees for me. Clear off the banks of the *oued*. I want to see water up and down stream. Pull up the grass. I don't want a single human being, animal, serpent, or scorpion from before to remain here. That also is a part of our holy war. Our holy war is just that!"

He divided the area into lots and called together the inhabitants of the former city.

"Bring your stones, only your stones. I want nothing that will corrupt Islam. Here my own Karouan will rise. Here will rise the first capital of the Muslim empire of the Occident. There will be others as long as I am on the march, *Allah akbar!* I will come back to inspect your work, of that you can be certain."

He did not bother to set up camp to supervise the initiation of the work. He knew very well that the spirit breathed only the length of time a spark endures, and that a spark risked oblivion before it had given birth to the smallest of embers. He had to give the Muslims a purpose while Islam was still in its dawn. However deeply they believed, men had need of a concrete faith, and of the works of their hands: battles or buildings.

As he pursued his way toward the setting sun, he measured the roadway already covered in so few years by the gallop of his steed as its hoofs pounded out space and time. Born a nomad, he had remained a nomad and no doubt would die as one when his hour came. He did not want to think for a single instant that the faith for which he mixed his breath with

God's would be sedentary one day, as though there were nothing more to discover, to create, to love, than the past . . . .

It was in the Aures Mountains, despite the quintain fever that was weakening him, where he was decimating the enemy with his own arms. (He bypassed the citadels and fell on the commandos of the Berbers of the *bled* with small groups of his own commandos.) There and then, Oqba heard the news: he had been stripped of his command. Ibn Moukhallad, the governor of Egypt on whom the army of Africa was dependent, had just replaced him with a certain Aboul Mouhajjir Dinar, a recently freed man promoted to the rank of general through intrigue. The messenger who brought the sealed dispatch had also brought the rumors of the secular court of Islam:

"Dinar is in the corridors of power. . . . He had been forced to wait around for a long time, without any great favors or appointments. . . . The prince wanted to recompense him. . . . The Caliph, the Prince of Believers, has no idea of any of this. . . . Most assuredly. He is in Damascus."

While the messenger spoke, Oqba looked at him without saying a word, just coughing. Then he put the palm of his hand on the messenger's chest and pushed him out of his mind.

"Dismount!" he shouted to his Bedouins.

With them, in the dust and brambles, he prayed the prayer of tenacity, prostrating himself in the direction not of Mecca, but of the Occident of which he had his visions day and night:

Lord, you are not only in the East, glory be to Thee!
You are also there where every evening You send the sun
    toward a well-determined goal!
Give me life, Master of the Rising and the Setting Sun,
So that I may sing Your praises and celebrate Your glory
To the very end of the world that You created.
Amen!

"Amen!" repeated the chorus of voices.

"Wait for me here," said Oqba when he arose. "Burrow yourselves into the grottos. There are plenty of them here in the mountains. I shall not be away for very long."

He was back in less than a month's time. The caliph had died a fine death, and so had the governor of Egypt. Another caliph had mounted the spiritual throne, and another master reigned in the palace on the banks of the Nile. As for him, he had been reinstated in his functions. He had even been honored with the title of Governor of North Africa for life. His eyes were no longer dilated with fever. He smiled, calmly. Behind him, he dragged along his prisoner, mounted and chained to a camel, a certain Aboul Mouhajjir Dinar, ex-general who had had the temerity to seek to follow in his footsteps and, even worse, had dared to imitate the voice of Islam in the base plots of the court.

2

Standing in his boat in the middle of the Oum-er-Bia one luminous morning in the spring of the year 681, Azwaw Aït Yafelman. He knows that the world is going to die, that another one is on the march to the pounding of hoofs, and that Oqba will be appearing in the hours to come. His couriers apprised him of the fact the night before, but he does not even glance toward the edge of the nearby forest above which, high in the sky, a falcon he has just loosed turns in circles.

It is at Yerma that he looks, as if she were the immediate future of his people. She is there, a short distance away, on the bank, pounding her washing on a white stone, surrounded by the colored droplets of water of every shade of flower of the field. Across the width of the river, he still desires her and calls her by name. She does not turn around. With her hair trickling water and her wet dress sticking to her body like a second skin, smoking under the rising sun, she straightens herself and throws back her head in a gesture of defiance. Mischievous and radiant, she begins the first notes of the song of fishing. She is not tired.

It is in the water, diving in and splashing with arms and legs, where he had taken her a while before with all his pagan strength. If he had spread a bit of his seed in the Oum-er-Bia, well then, let it sprout forth and engender the fish of tomorrow, in the sludge, in the gorse, creating as much life as it wants! And if some of the curious, males and females, crouched up and down the river to drink in with their eyes the aquatic frolics, so, let them do the same, the same prayer to life! They have their glands, in addition to their eyes and their envy. One by one, they went their way, almost regretfully.

Yerma swims back to the rock, to put her blood and her joy to use. "Li-la-la-la la-li-la la-la-la-la." He is proud of his daughter, almost as much as he is of himself: she is never tired. With every miscarriage, she starts again with more ardor. She smiles and says: "Next month, surely." Next month, she will be fourteen years old. It is a good age for her womb to be that of a woman, mature. Azwaw has foreseen everything, down to the minor details, so that she and he would be together forever, Oqba, Allah, or nothingness!

He is also proud of Hineb, his wife, who comes down the promontory toward him, carrying their naked infant son in her arms. When she gets to the edge of the river, she will bathe him as she does every sun-filled morning. Since her return, she has fire. Nothing of the dryness of other times. He takes her with pleasure, and how she eats!—she chews, she swallows, and she laughs. Yerma hardly speaks to her and often has a headache as night approaches. As he cannot cut himself in two or be in two beds at one time, Azwaw expends himself in one bedchamber after the other. He sleeps a short siesta in the afternoon, in a grotto that only he knows. There he collects himself and his ideas. He needs time to think sanely about public affairs and about the final details of his plan. Sometimes he awakens with a start, thinking that he hears a multitude of gallops, but no, it is only the ocean breaking against the rocks, in peace. One more day to wait.

Hineb still has narrow hips and small breasts. It is from these flanks no wider than a furrow between two rows of beans that Yerma and Yassin had come. He has forgiven her everything since she has "become a woman." And her milk flows in abundance. It was good, Azwaw had tasted it. Four months before she was pregnant, she had been told by Azoulay that she would have a son. He explained to her why she should name him Yassin, as a simple word could influence destiny. He had said . . .

It was two years earlier, the day after the oath in the Oum-er-Bia. It was midday. The synagogue was dug into the cliff, at the extreme point of the territory of the Yahouds. Its gate opened directly to the sea. On the cliff's walls, smooth and humid, a smoking oil lamp hung from a vault by three thin chains. A steel-blue sword, its tip thrust into the earthen floor, stood nearby. Along the wall facing the ocean, there was a stone table that looked like an upturned watering trough. A man older than age sat on a tripod near the sword. He was smaller than it was. He was so thin that he was almost without substance. His yellow beard spread out down beneath his knees. He was completely dressed in black, and his feet were bare. Without looking at Azwaw or moving his lips (he hardly had any), he said:

"So you are finally here, son. I have things to talk with you about."

His voice spat out the words and grated between syllables.

"This is Azoulay," explained Moushi in a soft voice. "He can barely move."

The old man's index finger rose slowly and pointed toward the door. Moushi the rabbi joined his hands in a sign of deference and went out. There was silence of all but the voices of the sea. Azoulay's eyes were absent, but soft and warm.

AZWAW: Where do you come from, creature? I have never seen you here before.

AZOULAY: Time is long. I come and I go, while time is hurried and men stray from the path. It would be better for you to ask me how I can help you.

AZWAW [*bending his knees and sitting cross-legged*]: Aha? You want to help me? *You*? Aha! [*His laughter is as raucous as the bellowing of a forge.*]

AZOULAY: You have torments. They are the same as those of my people. That is why I am here before you.

[*Pause.*]

AZWAW: [*abrupt in his intonation*]: I've been an orphan for a long time with this same grey beard you see, and it is not to say I'll have another father out of a grave to show me the way.
been a father, and I don't need to be told what path to follow.

AZOULAY: Yesterday you gave a destiny to your people, a sort of exodus that would be crowned by a reassembly. Moses could not have spoken better than you did, my son.

AZWAW: I am not your son, and I don't know that Moses.

AZOULAY: Moses had a God who guided him. You have none.

AZWAW: I am my own god.

AZOULAY: And you are also your own chieftain?

AZWAW: Neither god nor master.

AZOULAY: There is a Berber chieftain whose power extends from these lands to the land of Hannibal. His name is Gregory. You have made no call to him!

AZWAW: Only his skin is Berber—and still! [*Vehemently*]: His heart is Nazarene. He is in the service of the Christians. Do you call that a chieftain?

AZOULAY: Yes. A great one, following the appearance of the world. At least he was until recently.

[*Pause.*]

AZWAW: What do you mean, he was? What do you mean?

AZOULAY: He has just died. [*He stretches out one hand toward the handle of the sword, pulls it, and lets go of it. Then with a single twang, space resonated into one vast vibration to the limits of hearing. Resonances give birth to resonances, infintely, more and more intense. Azwaw gives a start, then takes hold of himself. The vibration has traversed his very bones. The old man has not budged an inch.*]

AZOULAY [*strangely, his voice at the same level, but very clear*]: In front of you, there is a barred window. Do not look out at the sea. Look at the sky. What do you see there?

AZWAW [*shouting to be heard*]: It's no use. There is nothing but blue sky. A spring sky. I saw it in its entirety before I came to this old man's tomb. You aren't impressing me.

AZOULAY: What do you see there *now*?

AZWAW: Look yourself.

AZOULAY: [*without turning around*]: A black cloud moves forward, stops, and then takes human form. The head is covered by a helmet, the chin is prolonged by a beard tailored to a point. Before the body there is a shield with an insignia on it: a lion with two heads. You recognise the insignia of King Joureir, don't you? You recognise his face that is found on coins, don't you?

[*There is a long pause during which Azwaw looks first at the sky and then at the man who is speaking. Then he gets to his feet and moves his fingers in front of Azoulay's eyes, which remain fully open, not blinking.*]

AZWAW: You are blind and yet you see!

AZOULAY: God called Moses to the mountain, and Moses complied. He did not see God, although he looked everywhere, but the Eternal One was there.

AZWAW: Keep your Eternal Ones and your Moseses for yourself. I'm not a Jew. I am a Berber and my name is Azwaw Aït Yafelman.

AZOULAY: If Moses had closed his eyes, he would have seen God.

[*Short pause.*]

AZWAW: That still does not concern me.

AZOULAY: Look at the sky once more. Tell me what you see.

AZWAW: Stop this rubbish!

AZOULAY: Look.

AZWAW: The cloud . . . [*suddenly stupefied*] . . . it is . . . it . . .

AZOULAY: It has turned red at the level of the throat, hasn't it? Now the head rolls off, detached from the trunk. It falls into the ocean. The cloud disappears, as all disappears except the future. Jourjir has just perished at the hands of an Arab soldier named Ibn Zoubaïr, near the city of Sbeitla. His army is in flight as I tell you this.

AZWAW: You know nothing. This is sorcery! Or I have barely spared myself these recent weeks.

AZOULAY: There is no sorcery. There is only destiny.

AZWAW: Listen, you: I know no destiny. I wonder how you were able to guess that there was a cloud, but from there to the nonsense you've been talking . . .

AZOULAY: The cloud takes the form of our thoughts, and our thoughts are no more than reflections of what we know or do not know about our destiny. Sit down, my son. I owe a great debt to your people. I am not here to convince you, but to help you.

[*He stretches out his hand and touches the hilt of the sword. The blade stiffens. The silence grows. Only the voice-like sound of the rising tide can be heard. One wave calls, and another responds. Hearing them, someone in the background sighs, but it is neither Azwaw nor Azoulay. Azwaw turns around and looks behind himself. The oil lamp has gone out.*]

AZOULAY [*in a toneless voice*]: At the beginning of history, the Berber people lived in the land of Palestine. They had a king named

Goliath. On this land lived the Hebrew people. Their king was named David. David killed Goliath. The Berber people emigrated and divided into tribes. Certain ones established themselves in Libya, others in Marmarique, and still others in the mountain regions. The tribe of the Louwata went as far as the Pentapole, the territory of the Barqa. It broke up in turn. Several families reached the territory where we are now, at the limit of the great river and the ocean. You are their descendant.

AZWAW [*becoming master of himself once again*]: And so? Life is life and death is death. You see history in your own light. We see it differently, from the other side: the earth. It is its history that counts, what happens to it, and not to the men who are only its sons and who come and go, here and there, like passing guests. They become attached to some little parcel of the earth or they disappear without any trace, depending on whether the nourishing mother loves them or rejects them. And so it is for plants and animals, for everything that the earth carries on her back. And I don't give a damn about Palestine, which is nothing but a little piece of earth!

AZOULAY: It was the paradise, the Garden of Eden.

AZWAW: That may be, but I don't give a damn. My own paradise is the Oum-er-Bia, the gardens and the fields that she bathes at her mouth, here and now, during my lifetime. I am not going to return to the cemetery of your time to get interested in that Goliath you speak of. My fingernail under my teeth. I haven't a damn thing to do with all that! [*He cracks his nail against his teeth to illustrate his point.*] You aren't going to ask me to take revenge on that old ancestor, are you? Besides, I never even saw him! . . . .

AZOULAY: Others have taken that responsiblity. The Christians razed Jerusalem, our holy city of which they only left one or two stretches of wall. And history has repeated itself. What you have known, we also have known, several centuries later. Our people have been scattered throughout the earth. Certain tribes have penetrated the desert of Libya, the Aures and the Atlas Mountains. A dozen families got this far. You have been very good to my people, severe but fair. I have a double debt to you. I came here to help you.

AZWAW [*syllable by syllable*]: With your weakness?

AZOULAY: Yes, with my weakness.

AZWAW: Granted. What could you do that I have not already done?

AZOULAY: You have brought nothing with you from your land of origin. We have. A great deal. In writing. All of our patrimony, everything that our ancestors knew. We are not numerous, but wherever we may be, we have arms with which to face life. That is what is called . . . our weakness.

[*For a long time Azwaw looks at him, as if he were studying a rare type of crabgrass. He suddenly becomes very attentive.*]

AZWAW: Speak on, grandfather. I'm listening to you.

AZOULAY: Recently there was a woman who crossed my path. She gave me her hand to guide me. She didn't say very much. Her hand spoke for her. When we walked by a certain tree, I pulled off a piece of bark and handed it to her. She chewed on it. You are happy with that woman now, are you not?

AZWAW [*with stifled exclamation*]: Hineb? Do you mean to tell me that—

AZOULAY: In a few weeks, she will be pregnant with your son. When this son is among us, call him by *another* name. By *their* name.

[*Complete silence.*]

AZWAW: What other name? What are you talking about? What are you up to with that old tongue of yours?

AZOULAY: Yassin: I came only to tell you that name. It is written in their book

AZWAW: What book?

AZOULAY: The one that put their people on the march. Don't you hear them coming at full gallop? Look! Turn toward the sky again. Look! [*He has bent his sword, but this time it is a heart-rending cry that is heard, a brief but very strong one. Then silence again.*]

AZOULAY: What is it that you see?

AZWAW: The sky . . . the . . . the river.

AZOULAY: Close your eyes. What do you deduce from what you have just seen?

AZWAW [*slowly; the words roll off his lips one after another like so many pebbles filling his mouth*]: Someone . . . you could say that . . . someone is calling . . . . It is . . . a cry of fear, but also a cry of deliverance.

AZOULAY [*in a very low, toneless voice, almost a whisper*]: That is it. Now you are making use of your own powers. Stay where you are. Do not turn around or even move. Keep your eyes closed and listen. You will name your son Yassin because in less than two years, someone will cry out his name, and it is precisely through that name that destiny will change, the destiny of your son like that of your people. [*In an urgent manner*]: No, do not turn around. Not yet. I am going to tell you what you are getting ready to ask me. Your own personal destiny will be very high, as high as the very sky. Remember that: as high as the very sky. And afterwards . . . afterwards, to the end of your life, you will no longer talk. Not another word.

Azoulay's voice died away quietly. The voices of the ocean returned little by little, filling the resonant space. Azwaw opened his eyes again and expelled the painful mass of air that swelled his lungs. The feeling of bewitchment that had paralyzed him despite his efforts to resist slowly faded away. He turned around with one single movement, his fists knotted, his veins spasmodic, protruding from his neck. The grotto was empty, completely empty. There was nothing of what he had seen so clearly, not even the stone altar or the oil lamp. Which portal opened onto the sea? Which barred window? *His* grottos, where he sometimes hid away, where everything was familiar to him, down to the pebbles—with the exception of a small hole in the soil which the point of a sword had formed.

When he was interrogated, Moushi the rabbi swore by the Eternal God and all the devils in hell that he had never led Azwaw to the synagogue, neither that day nor any other. Nothing could change his mind, neither threats nor blows. He called down maledictions on his descendants: let them be accursed to the seventh generation if he wasn't telling the truth of the very truth! No, by Yhw, no! He knew no one named Azou . . . . He pronounced half of the name Azoulay, and with fear, covered his face.

He named the boy Yassin. He did not know exactly why. He may have wanted to make certain that luck was on his side, even magic spells and dreams due to indigestion or the fast flow of his lovemaking.

It clearly is a son. He has no doubt of it. He is as proud as he can be. Already seven months. Hineb brings him to the river to bathe him. She undoes her long hair and wraps him in it to dry him. The child opens his mouth, his lips make a sucking movement, and a breast comes forth, immediately offering pearly drops of milk. In the distance is Yerma with her crystal song. Above and beyond his own desire, Azwaw sees it all: the milk of his wife, the clarity of her gaze, and the acute hunger of the life that is beginning. Everything is in place for the new world that is advancing like a human mountain. Oqba and his horsemen can come, and all the Muslims on the face of the earth! Azwaw does not feel the least concern. He awaits them.

He has fully utilized every day in the two years that have gone by since the oath-taking in the Oum-er-Bia. With the help of Boucchous who had spent time in Karouan and of several refugees who were "knowledgeable," he had learned Arabic, or very nearly. Above all, he had also learned several sourates of the Koran, and the most striking he could recite aloud. He could not distinguish one written letter from a tree, but with his Berber mind, he had carefully considered and meditated on the differences of their words and of one language from the other, the changes of meanings or similarities with regard to the earth and men. From mouth to ear, from the tribes of the Atlas Mountains to his tribe, he had sought information about the commander-in-chief of the Arab army; what he eats, how he sleeps and where, with whom, his lineage, his family to the seventh degree, his friendships, his strengths and weaknesses . . . . Consequently, Azwaw knows Oqba without ever having seen him.

He was invited in every house in the village, without drinking so much as a drop of water or eating a crumb of bread. He would go in, and would go back again, to remind the inhabitants of the plan, and to explain its ramifications, until the idea took form in their bodies and ran in their veins in place of blood. He had sent off various members of the community, twenty of the surest ones, both men and women, to install themselves in different areas, in the north, in the center of the country, high up in the Atlas Mountains, and down to the south in the Sousse, anywhere that the Aït Yafelmans had a cousin, a daughter-in-law, or any kind of relative.

These were the points of overthrow, that were to presage and prepare the event. He had left nothing to chance. It was as if he had sent the hand, a torso, a liver, or a rib from a body to the four cardinal points. You cannot kill a body whose parts are scattered in space and in time. Yes, indeed, let the Arabs come!

Standing in his boat, Azwaw awaits them. Everything is peaceful around him and inside him.

3

Dawn had surprised them with a battering rain. Like an arrow, two couriers had quickly gone the length of the two wings of the army, shouting out the orders of General Oqba:

"The Emir said: 'Paradise is before you and Hell is behind.' He has said: 'Do not stop under any pretext. Do not seek shelter under the cover of trees. Continue to follow the right bank of the river.' God watches over him and over you!"

The horsemen of Allah caught the water from the heavens in the outstretched palms of their hands and used it for their ablutions. Meanwhile, Hamza the muezzin, standing upright on his horse with his bridle drawn taut to maintain his equilibrium, called out the first prayer of the day in his stentorian voice. Erect in his stirrups at the head of his troops, Oqba cried out with all his strength, his soul sparkling and washed by the benediction-rain from the sky:

> *Let man consider how his subsistance comes to him!*
> *This is how. We have poured out water to overflow;*
> *Then we plowed the earth into furrows . . .*

Behind him, rank by rank, like waves of faith hurled at a gallop, the Bedouins took up the verses of the Book:

> *. . . the earth into furrows.*
> *We have caused grain to grow and grapes*
> *And date trees and olive trees*
> *And luxuriant gardens:*
> *Thus have you come onto the earth.*

They said their prayers on horseback, without slowing their march. Waterspouts fell on their heads like bolts of lightning from the sky. The water flew up in sprays under their horses' hoofs. All of those trees! So much verdure! The Atlas Mountains, with their arid climate and murderous ambushes, were behind them. When they had reached the passes through the Atlas, Oqba had designated a point in the steep cliff and said:

"There! I want to descend there."

And thus it was: a man bent over on the edge of a platform, far away from the war; above him, the Roumyat Mountains, looming some two thousand meters high, calcareous and bare, without a tree or a bush except for several thickets of boxwood from which squirrels playing in the rocks shot out like so many projectiles; from one peak to another, two wild sheep chased each other in a game of love and aerial leaps. The golds, ochres, siennas and, amethysts of the rising sun; and on the left, a peak held a single white egg, as big as a melon, that would become a vulture in a few seasons. Below the cliff, descending straight down, an abyss of voices: from the loins of the mountain in heat, its semen strong and roaring, burst forth with all the force of age a spring of green water into a cataract, Mother Spring.

For a long, long time, Oqba had contemplated all of that, had listened and meditated on this dawn of creation. Then he had said:

"I want that! I want that river. We are going to follow it. It will take us to its end, to the end of the earth. That I know."

Whatever the stakes, he had refused to join in battle ever since. It was as if the enemy were henceforth nothing more than an army of ants, and their citadels, nothing more than ant hills that weren't worth even a simple breath. His eyes riveted to the setting sun, Oqba ibn Nafi felt the frenzy of those last days surge and beat in his veins. Soon, even tomorrow, *incha Allah*, he would unfold the green banner of the Prophet. His eyelids and his forehead were seamed with an infinity of lines, and his face was the color of leather from looking at the sun.

Under a lean-to near the port, Wasok the blacksmith works with the mass, and hammers a long bar of copper held up by blocks of stone, as wide as a man's step and as thick as an arm. He doesn't hear or see anything, neither the blows of metal on metal nor the sparks that surround him. The noise has passed over his ears for a long time now. As for the points of fire that fly by his eyes, they are only fugitive. He has been shaping and finishing the prow of the boat that Azwaw requested for more than a month. He loves copper, hot or cold, and the odor of charcoal and cow-dung that prolongs the life of the embers. He loves his work. Naked and sweating under his leather apron, he pounds away from morning to night. Azwaw has told him: "Take your time. No hurry."

Several woodsmen with axes cut off branches of trees that lie side by side on the wharf. As they cut them up, the bark flies up in oak spirals, wooden blades, and chips. They fasten a hook to the trunks and attach a cord. Then, with the cord over their shoulders, they pull the thick planks the length of the ship. Their movements are disjointed, but regular and slow. If they talk at all, it is about the present moment or about the grain that is growing or the cows that are calving down below in the fields. Almost straight up and cutting the azure sky is a mast on whose tip a man is buttressed, rocked by the rhythm of the rising tide. Only he hears what he is singing as loud as he can, up there high above the sea. Methodically, he finishes polishing the mast with a piece of millstone.

The millstone grinds joyously in the mill, filling up almost all the space. Everything is whitened and perfumed with the barley powder to the innermost recess. The vanes of the mill squeak and groan as the waters of the Oum-er-Bia engulf it. A stone's throw away, in the open air, stands a press made of argan-tree wood, as hard as granite. From time to time, two strong men grasp an arm of the vise and give the screw a turn. The sharp odor of olive oil arises and is carried in waves by the sea breeze toward the hills, as the oil itself noiselessly flows into the cask, black and thick, with occasional flames the color of honey whenever a ray of sunlight dances on it.

A line of women on the riverbank pass plates of red earthenware, heavy and fragile, from one to another. They are still cool, having just dried under the light of the moon. From mid-morning to mid-afternoon, they must be exposed to the sun, so that they will be hardened eternally. It is back again, hot and luminous as joy, after the torrential rain of the day before. In three or four weeks, they will bury them in the ground, in vaults where the charcoal is made. The fire will make them sparkle.

At regular intervals, a woman examines a plate that has just been passed to her, bends her back to pick up a bit of wet clay from between her feet, rubs it into the crack, fissure, or defect with her finger, and then polishes it, spits on it, and polishes it again.

Further on, amid the sound of voices, a group of young women, crowned with the jocose aureoles of their laughter, dip their arms up to the elbow in a jar that is almost as tall as they, pull out long strips of meat dripping with juice and odors, and stretch them out on a string. The string forms a triangle whose angles are trees: a maple, a birch, and a sycamore. They are all flowering, with yellow-green or purple flowers that the grandmothers of the tribe gathered as soon as they blossomed and crushed them with certain barks and roots to make a mixture with sea water in which to marinate the meat for a long time. They know the secrets of the good things of life. Dried under the great sun, the meat can be kept intact in the open air for more than a year.

On the prairie beside the hill, the grass is tender and green with the raw verdure of life. There is not a calf, not a ruminant in sight. Standing, Raho slowly looks around the horizon. There is not a bump or a hole. Azwaw had said: "I do not want arms in the city. We have no need for them." Raho had gathered them all together and buried them. The grass found its path. It must go on growing. Time will do the rest. The earth is a good guardian.

Between ocean and river, at the intersection of their roiling waters, a flamingo has suddenly turned its head toward the forest, surprised by something it still does not hear. With wings partially open, it stands there an instant, frozen like a rose-colored statue, then relaxes and begins to dig about in the sludge of the riverbed. All around are other birds, and up above, invisible in the brilliance of the light, a falcon turns in silent flight.

In the quarter of the Yahouds, Schloumou closes one book and opens another which he hands to the rabbi. His eyelids have no lashes and he does not read quickly, but of what he does read, not a word will be lost until his death. And, from now until then, he will be able to transmit and to restore to future generations all the books he has read, exactly as he has read them, page by page and sign by sign. The writings of a people can be lost or go up in smoke—that has already been proven by the events of history. For the tribe of the Yahouds, Schloumou is a living memory. He has been reading without stop for two years. Moushi the rabbi piles up the books one by one, with care, under a flagstone that he will seal off soon. No doubt tomorrow. Certain manuscripts are as old as time itself.

On the door of the house of Azwaw, the necklace of cock feathers has been removed and two date palms, which an Aït Yafelman picked in a desert in the south, have been nailed up in its place. In the patio, a jug of milk and a basket of fresh dates have been awaiting the visitor for several days. They are renewed every morning. Not an inhabitant of the dwelling touches them. Azwaw had said: "It is their custom. That is the way in which they receive their guests of Islam."

Naked, Yassin paddles about in the water, laughs a bit, and cries a bit. Hineb holds him under the armpits. She always gives him a second bath after his feeding. The Oum-er-Bia is good for indigestion, for the skin, and for all sorts of illnesses that stalk a child. Suddenly a dark cloud passes between her and Yassin. She looks up and sees the falcon that has just fallen like a stone into the boat at Azwaw's feet. The sun is oblique and blinding. She cannot see Azwaw very well, nor discern the look on his face. She does clearly hear his voice, however. Why would he cry out with such vehemence to Hineb at that very instant? She does not recognize that voice. Is it Azwaw's? From far away, even before it materialises, an ancient, almost forgotten fear surfaces . . . .

General Oqba ibn Nafi raised his arm. Behind him, thousands of horses broke their four-hooved trot, instantly. Before him was God's music: the sea.

And so it was: before the image that filled his eyes, there was the emotion of the image, projected like a soul; before all sound, the emotion of sound. A wave came from the depths of the ocean and of time, and slowly, rolling forward with power, it burst into foam, charged with Islam. It exploded, blasting every reality of man. Another wave followed on top of the first and struck like lightning, sparkling and streaming with new life. Nameless and overflowing the banks of humanity, from eternity to eternity, other waves were born, covered one another, and renewed one another, adding their life to life. From however far off one heard them, they all had the same voice, repeating the same word: *peace, peace, peace* . . . And so it was: the joy of joy decomposed Oqba's visage and reached the very marrow of his bones. Stammering, he said:

"Naquishbendi . . .send . . . send for Naquishbendi."

His voice was so broken by sobs that he had to repeat himself several times. All of his horsemen had dismounted around him and wept without tears or sound. Their horses puffed and snorted.

No one would have given a dime to the man who came to stand in front of the commander-in-chief. He looked gray, dressed in gray, had no expression on his face, and had the hands of a peasant farmer. He took the reins of Oqba and wrapped them around his waist. He did nothing else, and did not say a word. If he had been born one day long ago in Damascus, if he had lived on earth sixty-five years and accompanied Oqba all the way from the desert of Tripoli, it was only for that very instant.

"Naquishbendi, my brother," Oqba said to him. "For the love of God, play for us. Give to God and to us the soul of your hands."

Naquishbendi gave a timid smile. His lute hung down his back. He slipped it down his left shoulder with the tender gesture of handling a sleeping infant. Not once had he looked at the sea. He gazed questioningly into Oqba's eyes, tears streamed down his cheeks, the savage splendor of his faith, his fatigue, his past and future doubts, the dust encrusted in his skin, turned his beard and eyebrows to clay.

Mud came up to his horse's breast like a shell. He saw and understood the end of the earth and of the war, the triumph of man, and perhaps of God. One instant he closed his eyes in order to gather into his body all of his quivering sensations and make them descend into his hands. When he opened his eyes again, his fingers were already running over the strings in a series of bounds to which his heart responded like a needle to a magnet. Thus:

And so it was from the edge of the forest to the last mouth of the Oum-er-Bia, to the very union of earth and ocean: notes of carnal emotion amplified by their resonances. Thus:

The general was nothing more than a man named Oqba the son of Nafi, seated on his saddle, his legs stiff, his body shaken by convulsive shudders, and his eyes straight ahead. His horse got into step, pulled by another man who slowly walked backward and who was nothing more than pure music. Fingers of flesh and blood suddenly changed, by the grace of music, into traces of fire that transformed the strings of the lute into a burst of sonorous light. The artist no longer had identity or life: his life was present in that assemblage of pieces of wood that is called a lute in the language of words. And he continually stared into Oqba's face, as if to ask, "Are you well? Why does your joy make you suffer? Wait . . . Wait . . ." He shook his head, humbly, and all of a sudden, with a change of scales, he made a half-tone note resound with the power of a thousand explosions.

Ten thousand pairs of eyes were riveted to the sight of the sea, and listening to each drop of the waves crashing with their intense beauty. Each Bedouin walked in front his horse with a grave and absent air, as if the time of the old world had come to an end, and the dawn of a new time was on the rise. All of them felt within themselves the hands of Naquishbendi. No one could have said what it was that he was playing. Even he did not know, but what he was trying to do was to interpret God, and the men and the earth that the Creator had given to them as their cradle. Sometimes when Naquishbendi marked a pause at the top of a musical elevation, a shout that sprang from ten thousand hearts resounded:

"*Allah akbar!*"

Feet and hoofs cut through the branches and bushes, trampled the grass, and flattened the pebbles and sand. As far as they could be heard, voices and footsteps echoed the same word: glory.

At the mouth of the river, near Yerma, a crow with scarlet legs perched on a white rock. Right wing raised, it picked around with its yellow beak, then suddenly took off in vertical flight, ahead of any perceived human sound. That was the signal. The sky was instantly filled with the beating of wings. No more birds on the Oum-er-Bia's banks.

Up on the hillside, studying the grass, Raho was the first to hear the Arabs and their music and chants. Then he saw them come out of the forest in closed ranks, followed by their horses. He did not budge any more than a rock. None of them gave him so much as a glance. He vaguely wondered why. They went by him as though he were merely a tree trunk.

Schloumou closed the last book, kissed it, and then held it out to Moushi the rabbi. The two of them, short of breath, pushed the flagstone back into place with all their strength. The tallow-smelling candle was snuffed out. The grill closed on the vault of the cemetery where the two men had stood guard for two years. Everything was consummated for the century of centuries.

A woman let a strip of meat drag on the steep river bank. Immediately she dipped it into the water to wash away the sand. Another woman almost dropped a plate that her neighbor had just passed on to her, but she got hold of herself, got hold of it, and took up the rhythm of the chain again. Why were these warriors marching in procession? Whom were they burying? Why were they, and why was their leader, weeping? Slowly, one foot placed before the other, one foot after the other, they continued straight on their way, as if the line of women were no more than a row of stones as inanimate as the earthenware plates they held.

In Wasok's forge, which had once been a deafening uproar of hammering mass against a copper ship's stem-post, there was now only a barely perceptible murmur in the midst of the ample chanting that was now almost continuous: *"Allah akbar!"* Such was the flux and reflux, that the two words, united into a single word, descended from the first rank of soldiers to the last, and then rippled forward again with the same fervor. A horse detached itself from the multitude, trying to find its master.

"Destiny. Do you know what destiny is? And who will ever tell you what destiny is?"

He ordered two deaths. No doubt pushed by thirst, Hamza, the muezzin's horse, went toward the river, precisely to the place where Hineb was. At exactly the same moment, she stretched out her arms to pick up and protect her son. Until then she had not been afraid. Azwaw had told her repeatedly in various ways to fear nothing and no one. He was over there in the middle of the Oum-er-Bia calling out her name with his cast-iron voice: "Hineb! . . . Hineb!," more and more violently as he approached her, cutting through the water with his oars. What did he want to tell her? She had turned her back to him to watch the Arabs go by, her curiosity almost peaceful. Her hand firmly held Yassin's hands as he joyously paddled about in the water. It was not until the horse was right upon her and reared up, its mouth cut by its bit (Hamza had caught up with it at a racing pace, had grabbed the reins and pulled on them), with a terrifying whinny, that she lived out the end of her childhood.

Things she had completely put out of her mind suddenly came back to her, more vivid than in real life. What time and two maternities had, in a sense, covered over with verdure and flowers, was there once again, as harsh and naked as the cruelty of former times, with a pitiless sense of detail. Her mother falls to her knees. She holds out her arms to her and calls her by name: "Hineb!" A stream of foaming blood bursts from a hole at the height of her breast. On horseback, straight in his stirrups between bed and hearth, a man with eyes more flaming than hot coals has just pulled a reddened sword out of the wound. He twirls it whistling in the air, drops of blood spattering about, before swinging it downward like an ax. The head rolls onto the earth with a sound as clear and full as from a headman's block, the mouth still open, forming the cry hardly made: "Hineb!" Then, the still-convulsing torso is crushed under the multitude of hoofs, trampling everything underfoot, as wattles burst and the roof comes falling down, while outside the air is filled with the tremendous chant of triumph: *"Allah akbar!"*

That morning of the year of grace 681, surmounting space, time, solitude, and suffering, a woman dropped the hands of her son and held out her arms to him in one single and unique gesture, one single and unique cry: "Yassin!" This word had an immediate effect: two almost simultaneous deaths, and, in the days and centuries to follow, a projection on all the Berber people. It changed their destiny.

It was in a scream that rose from the very depths of her past that she stridently cried out the name of her son, into the nostrils of the horse that began to neigh and kick, and that threw its master down onto the white stone. A spine broke. The muezzin's trajectory was not yet over when another trajectory came to its term: an arrow had penetrated Hineb's throat, cutting the jugular vein, of which the Koran speaks in a shining verset: "God is closer to you than your own jugular vein." Hineb died surrounded by the chants of the Muslims. It was then that she knew why, as a terrified child in the midst of the desolation that had descended on her village one far distant dawn, she had wept with joy; and, at the very moment she knew it, she ceased to know.

A detachment left the procession in sections. Soldiers, ready to exterminate anything that moved, were deployed along the length of the river. There were Berbers that came out of nowhere, and Yerma who dove in to save the infant. Azwaw, already swimming between two waters and possessed with all the fury of a cave man, stirred up a veritable white whirlpool. Those Arabs who had heard the resounding word—Yassin—hesitated to unsheath their swords or to ready their bows. They talked among themselves and stopped the movements of their arms. A courier flattened himself against the earth and cried:

"Sons of Islam, listen! The Emir has said: 'No more dead!' He said: 'I do not want my peace troubled any more!' He said: 'Save the infant or you will answer with your head. Dress him. Take the immodest nubile girl and cover her with a decent mantle. Protect both of them in the name of Islam, and then bring me the man who was in the boat a little while ago.' That is what the Emir said, God keep him, and God keep you!"

Oqba had ordered the beach to be cleared. Very slowly, in the silence of men and the symphony of the waves, he went into the sea until the water was up to his horse's chest. He splashed his face and his neck three times with water and said "Allah" three times in a soft voice. Afterward, looking toward the rising tide, he spoke to Him who had set him in motion from the land of the Hegira:

"Lord of all the earth, of all the sea and men, I take You as my witness: this is the end of the earth, glory be to Thee! Your reign is once again what it was at the beginning. Once more, it extends from the Orient where You had me born into Islam, as far as this setting sun where I proclaim Your glorious sublime name, glory be to Thee! I am no more than one of Thy servants, but I take Thee as witness: I cannot go ahead. If I could find passage through the waters, I would pursue my ride to conquer the sea."

The green standard of the Prophet lay across his saddle. He unfurled it and planted its pole into the ocean. The water rose beneath him, and emotion inside of him, and he let it rise. His voice was almost cracked when he shouted as loudly as he could:

"*Yahya al-Islam!* Long live Islam!"

He stayed there, a sentinel in the sea, in a fit of coughing, while the Bedouins, standing on the rocks, perched on the roofs and in the trees like flags, took up and chanted the cry continuously:

"Long live Islam! *Yahya al-Islam!*"

Flying on its back, a black and white lapwing, with spots of squirrel red, descended from the zenith and returned to its perch on the riverbank, among the reeds where it was born. Perhaps it was deaf. Perhaps also it had flown so high up in the sky that it had seen what men on the ground could not yet see. Its crest still trembling, it let out a long modulated whistle. It was like a signal. Hundreds of thousands of wings pierced the air; the people of the birds once again took possession of their country, the Oum-er-Bia.

First Surah of the Koran

4

It is the most beautiful day of my life. This morning *Cadi* Zwitten offered me a copy of the Koran, done in Egypt, in calligraphy with intense black letters and green ornamentations. He said to me:

"*Imam* Filani I am giving to you what the Prince of Believers gave to me. It is very little considering who you are. I thank you for being who you are. I thank you for your voice, beautiful and immense. It alone has brought Islam to every horizon."

He, the most powerful man of the city, kissed my hand, that very aged hand full of wrinkles which everybody seizes and kisses with veneration. I opened up the Book. The first page leapt out at my eyes . . . . I caressed it for a long time, without reading even a single word. There is no need to understand. The sight of it is sufficient. Written as they are, the words descended from the heavens have become a garden. Their song is my daily song. It inhabits my soul and guides my steps.

It is like this garden that I walk through to go to the mosque. From the first to the last flower, all bear the same dazzling witness under God's sun: the human being can be sublime—and the work of his hands sublime. With their simple language of fragrances and colors, they address themselves to my whole life, to the man I was in other times and to what I shall be tomorrow *God willing* I truly do not know what to answer them. They are too pure, and a part of me, *Imam* Filani, is still impure.

I often sit in front of a clump or a bed of purslains, jasmins, or Peruvian marvels . . . or a quantity of other flowers whose names I don't know, that are just whatever they are. Do they really need a name to exist? I look at them, listen to them, and dream of them. They help me to meditate on the event, the advent that transformed this land in such a short period of time.

Thirty years have hardly gone by since the day that Oqba ibn Nafi went into the ocean on his horse. The men and women of my country no longer have to belong to a tribe or clan to survive. Islam, a greater community, has welcomed them to its breast, that spreads ever more widely before their descendants. Several of my brothers, solitary like myself or in groups, squat to admire them in silence. They also have gone beyond their name. That is the greatest prayer, the only one that is harkened to. Without patronym, without constraints, they approach one another henceforth from sun up to sun down, one Muslim to another, simply saying: "I come to you in God's name." There are no more doors. Souls are open.

What city is this I am in? I neither know nor care.

Cities were built or reconstructed so that their inhabitants would show solidarity and flourish. However small, every house is open to the sky, and has an inner garden and a room reserved for a guest. The doors are open day and night. However isolated they may be, every town has its mosque, as much for prayer as for meetings of the human community. And there are public gardens where water sings, and the music of all sorts of instruments brought from the Orient sings, and there are dances at popular festivities: the feast of sacrifice, circumcision, the birth of the Prophet, engagements, weddings, the departure or arrival of a caravan, the twenty-seventh night of the month of Ramadan, the night of Destiny . . . . That is where people spend the better part of their time, and above all swarms of children, of those children which I *so much would have liked to have had!* Even the cemetery is a garden. A marvel.

I go from town to town at the mercy of the history that calls me, and I rally the people with the only thing that has not grown old in me: my voice. That voice earlier brought me the friendship of Oqba, then the protection of the generals that followed him, and the honors that I now receive and which I use to the profit of my people.

I followed the army. Sometimes I even preceded it. I have been clear to the other side of the Atlas Mountains, then I came back down toward the south, and went back up toward the north. I must be in Tangier now, since there are two seas here. Everywhere I have gone, I have done only one thing: cry out the prayer from the top of the minaret, as only I can do it. And everywhere I have gone, I have found myself at home because, even in the smallest village, I have heard an echo of my voice: time. *That I know.*

At first I traveled on foot. I was young then, barely half a century old. Now that I am nearing my eightieth year, a carriage with a dais to protect me from the heat of the sun and pulled by four horses has been put at my disposition. God is good to his servants. He recompenses whom He wills, according to his merits. And following the great people of this world who have opened their arms to me as brothers, I have been worthy of Islam, very worthy. Oh, God is great.

Without my realizing it, a little cloud darkens the fragrant flowerbed before which I am sitting, then goes on its way. A flower is blossoming before my eyes . . .

If I were to return one day to my native town, would I recognize the voices of other times, or the odors and basic sensations that nourished me like no fire on earth? Passing friends or hosts tell me that it has changed, but no more than I. Much less, no doubt. It is that, the event. That is Islam. Souls have been transformed more quickly and more profoundly than stones. And yet, my soul was of granite, without mercy or faith in anything of this world. Who knows where I shall die? Perhaps on the edge of a road, in full combat. War is no longer between the Berbers and Allah's horsemen, but strangely enough between each Muslim and himself. I am myself in the bosom at the summit of Islam. That I know. Every day bears witness to that.

No, by God, it is not toward the cradle or distant childhood that I want to return, but toward a closer past, one that is still very much alive for me: the middle of the day of the year 681, at the mouth of the Oum-er-Bia. It is there, at that very instant, when everything began. Oqba ibn Nafi had just come out of the sea and put his foot onto the earth. I had known him for a long time. I had followed most of his conquests. I was standing before him I, the *imam* Filani. The man who had troubled his peace and his triumph, a barbarian named Azwaw, all covered with mud and smelling of fish, had been brought to him. They looked at each other in silence, without blinking an eye, either one of them, for the space of time of a birth or a death. I heard every one of their words. *I was a witness.* Thirty years later, I still am. How could I ever forget?

The houses had been vacated of all their inhabitants, even the animals. In front of them, a soldier, who mounted an imperturbable guard, was ready to raze them to the ground, if given the order. Or to go inside as a friend. One or the other, nothing in between. A spear was driven into the door; a sabre flashed through the air, higher than the roof; and the horse stood unmoving, covered with dust. Here and there, a Bedouin hastened to raise his desert veil up to the level of his eyes.

An officer circled in place, his horse's hoofs sounding on the cobbled street that went from the port to the dead end, in the Jewish sector. He held his hands to his mouth and trumpeted:

"Jewish men, Jewish women, Jewish children, stay in your homes! Stay in your homes! Go on living just as you have up to this day, and await orders."

Chasing off the few horsemen who came that far, he said:

"The Emir has said, 'They are believers. They have a god. Leave them in peace, unless they start a war against us one day.' He said, 'These are people of the Book. They are inscribed in our Book.' That is what the Emir said. May God keep him! Half-turn! And may the All-Merciful and our commander-in-chief show you mercy."

Dressed in black, with a black skull-cap, Moushi, a fragile silhouette that was almost a shadow of the immense shadow of the horse, had dared to approach him. Holding two white hends tied foot to foot under his arm, and a basket of eggs, he patiently tried to capture the attention of the officer. For a long time, he moved his lips in silence. Finally, he said:

"Sir Muslim, I . . . I would like to see your leader."

"Sir Jew, go back home."

"I . . . I am the rabbi."

"Go home, Rabbi."

Moushi had prepared another word, perhaps weeks or months earlier, but suddenly his mouth stayed wide open, without the least bit of sound. The two Arabs pushing Azwaw with the points of their spears went between him and the officer. For a moment, Moushi looked at the cackling fowls that struggled under his arm, but he did no more than look at them, as if they did not belong to him. When he took up a semblance of dialogue again, it was with a totally different voice, that of Destiny.

"My people and I . . ." he began.

"You're still there?" shouted the other, his sabre unsheathed. "For the third time, I tell you: go home."

"You can kill me later on, but in the meantime, let me ask what I came to ask of your leader: his protection for my people."

"Ask it of me. I am a Muslim like him."

"In the name of all my people, I want to go swear allegiance to your leader in person."

"My leader in person does not deign to cast the slightest look from between his eyelashes on the princes of this world who beg at his feet. And so, as for you! . . . . Get back to your synagogue."

Moushi was tenacious in his good will, and perhaps in his hope. He showed the eggs and the hens. He smiled humanely.

"It's not very much," he said, as if to excuse himself. "Will you please give these offerings to your chief, Sir Muslim? As a sign . . . a sign of welcome, *shalom*?"

"*Shalom*," answered the officer in a quiet voice. "Take back your unclean birds. The Emir does not like meat. Give me the eggs!"

He lifted up the basket, very high, and then let it fall. He shouted out the following syllables:

"WE HAVE NOT COME HERE TO EAT!"

Then off he went at a trot, dry and half-starved, to his squadron at the port. The small boats were now on the docks with their keels in the air. Those that were still in the water were quickly attached to the pommels of saddles, and, hocks stretched taut, the horses pulled.

Higher up, on the outskirts of the town, a detachment had surrounded the fields and was slowly rounding up the cattle in a human enclosure. Another detachment, split into two moving files, was directing the last stream of male Aït Yafelmans still in possession of their thirty-two teeth toward the beach. Some two thousand of their brothers were already on the sand, sitting in silence. A lieutenant had raised his voice:

"Stay seated! Respect the Emir's meditation, may God keep him!"

A sky-blue tent, surmounted with the standard of the Prophet, had been set up facing the sea. On the threshold stood Oqba's horse. Two grooms had removed its saddle and were giving it a vigorous rubdown. There were traces of hoofs between him and his master. At the edge of the last fringe of foam, where he had stepped onto the earth, Oqba stood, his back to the humans. Mute except in him, his prayer of thanksgiving mounted to the rhythm of the rise of the waves.

A long time later, a man came toward us. He was small and weak, with a sparse beard, and so wet up to the waist that I looked at him with stupor. He seemed so unthreatening on foot! He passed by my side without looking at me, without looking at any of us. The first person to whom he spoke was his friend, the horse. He embraced him and said:

"Seven of your brothers died under me in combat. May God keep their souls in paradise! If you speak beyond life to them or if you join them before I do, tell them to keep a small place for me near to them. Tell them that we have finally come to the end of the earth, you and I."

He suddenly turned around and shouted an order:

"Bring the man!"

"Forward, you!" stormed a voice. "On your knees!"

"No," said the Emir. "Let him stand! Let him speak to me standing!"

Azwaw had not said a word since some hands had pulled him by the ankles out of the river. He said not a word when a soldier had covered Yerma with a mantle and had thrown her howling over his horse. Not a single one at the sight of his son being plucked up by several arms, dried off, calmed down, dressed, and taken off at a gallop as well. Hineb's body floated a moment through the mist of his eyes and on the surface of the water; then the whirlpool swallowed it up at the foot of the black cliff. He did not even give a single glance at the corpse of Hamza that was being carried off on a bier of branches. He was a stranger.

Azwaw's eyes were wide open and fixed on that being that he could have broken in two with one hand. He still said nothing. He was waiting. Oqba was waiting too. The sun now gave no shade above their heads.

Who was the first to speak? I was present, very close to them, within touching distance, me, the *imam* Filani. My memory is older than I am. I think it was one and then the other at just about the same time. What I still remember is the Berber tongue that Oqba suddenly used. He said:

"A little while ago as I was going along the river, a woman was killed. Who was that woman?"

"My wife," said Azwaw.

"Before she died, she cried out a name: the name of a child we saved from drowning. Who is that child?"

"My son."

"Why that name?"

Azwaw called upon all that he had learned of the Koran in two year's time. With his full cast-iron voice, he recited the verses well known in the world of Islam:

"*Yà-Sin Qor'ani al-hakim!* Yes: you are one sent by the Lord, for a determined goal, in order to inform a people whose ancestors had not been informed and who until now has remained in ignorance and error . . ."

Then he was silent. (Briefly and violently, a chill ran straight down through his body, from his head down to his feet. He saw an extremely old man, blind, sitting in a grotto. Before him was a sword stuck in the earth . . . the clouds . . . the name . . .)

Oqba smiled. Under his beaked nose, his teeth were big, uneven up to the gums. He said:

"Your tongue is good, but what it sings does not correspond to the fear in the depths of your eyes. What are you afraid of?"

"Not of you."

"Of what then?"

"Of God. I venerate Him and I fear Him."

"Ha!" approved the still-smiling Oqba. "You belong to the religion?"

"Yes," answered Azwaw, sincere in his lying. "I am a Muslim like you. That is why my people did not take up arms against you."

"Ha!" repeated the Emir forcefully. "And how did that happen? When did you become a Muslim? Explain it to me. I am listening to you."

"The faith came to me. With reports of your glory."

Oqba waved his hand as if to chase away a fly. He said:

"Let it go. I am insensitive to all the winds, even those of the desert. They bring the wind, and you, you only bring words of wind. Those arms you were talking about a moment ago, tell me, was it you who furnished them to the Snassen and to the Cherarda that I found on my way and whom I vanquished to the very last man? Speak up! I am listening to you."

Azwaw did not hesitate a moment before speaking:

"That was before. Every man has the right to defend his lands. But . . ."

"Wait," said Oqba without raising his voice.

"No," replied Azwaw. "I will not wait! I am speaking to you man to man. Yes, at first, because I did not know, I tried to defend my land and my people with my mind, from afar, to try to put the other tribes between you and me. That is true. I admit it. What would you have done, you, if I had invaded your territory with an army of Berbers?"

"Me? Nothing. And you, you should have taken to the desert. But go on. Get all of your fear out of you."

"I am not afraid."

"Get it out anyway."

"You came," said Azwaw, suddenly very humble. "It is you who are right. *Allah akbar!*"

"Yes, Allah is greater than all of us!" retorted Oqba with the same tone of humility. "And tell me: did you convert to Islam just before I arrived?"

"I thought about it a great deal, not just for months, but for years. And as a consequence? I entered God's religion."

"As a consequence? By the horse's tail? All by yourself? Ha! . . ."

If anyone heard Oqba ibn Nafi's laughter that day, it was I, the *imam* Filani. It was a full-throated laugh, as broad as the sunlight that bathed us all.

"You see," said the Emir, "I know all the winds just as I know men, whether they come from the desert, the mountains, the plains or the sea. You are no Muslim."

These were his words, and the manner in which he pronounced them—a dense, warning silence, without recourse, between the words:

"You—are—no—Muslim! But—you—will—be—, thanks—to—me! And—your—people—will—be—also—thanks—to—you."

He began to cough. He stopped the last gasps of it and added:

"One does not use the word of the Book of Allah, not the least one, by way of currency, of politics or merchandising as you have just done here in front of me. I ought to kill you . . . and put to the sword those thousands of barbarians on the beach awaiting their fate.

"Kill all of us! We are prepared," cried Azwaw.

"No," said Oqba. "I have life for you. Do you want to know why?"

No one among us replied. *Not even I.*

"A word echoed in my soul: the name of your son. Yassin."

"Where is . . ."

"Wait! The first surah that I memorized in my childhood begins with the words: 'Yâ-Sîn! Wal Qor'ani al-hakim!' "

His voice broke. I looked up at him. Thirty years later, a whole lifetime later, I still do not comprehend how a fissure had opened up in me, at that very moment, into which the intense emotion of this man entered. In the meantime, Azwaw went toward him, grasped his hand, and kissed it. He said:

"Give me something of your friendship."

"I give it to you willingly at present, but remember this: in Islam, friendship is without false oath."

"Where is my son?"

"There where he is. Under our protection to his last breath, because of his name. We are all witnesses. That is our mission, our holy war."

"He is a hostage?"

"No. By God, no! Quite simply, he has not yet had the time to be contaminated. His destiny will be very great. I, Oqba ibn Nafi, affirm it."

"Will I see him again one day?"

"*Incha Allah!* God willing."

"If you have made these decisions for my fate, I, a defeated man, can do nothing."

"No, nothing. Not a whit or an iota."

Azwaw lowered his head. He had not asked for news of Yerma, but he would find her again, word of honor of Azwaw Aït Yafelman. Yassin also. Despite the distress that continued to reverberate throughout his body, he swore the oath. When he raised his eyes, he saw that Oqba was looking in the direction of the promontory.

"Is that your house?"

"Yes, and it is yours also. It awaits you."

"I don't want a house. My tent is fully enough for me. Do you know the words of the call?"

"Yes. I worked at it for two years."

Oqba smiled once more.

"It is good to feel naked, without falsehood, isn't it?"

"Yes. I'm not struggling any more, and all of my life has been a struggle."

"Then go climb to the roof of your house and give the call to prayer, in the interim, until a minaret is added to it. Give your call in that direction (he held out his arm to indicate the other side of the river). That is where I shall construct the New City."

His smile grew wider before he added:

"Your people are waiting there and understanding nothing. I have not had them assembled for no reason. Tell them that I am going to raze the city here. It is pagan to its very foundations. It is the very soul of the battle that you expected to wage against us Arabs. Against me, Oqba, the son of Nafi of the desert! I have known this for a long time, well before I came across the Atlas Mountains. You, who are now my friend in Islam and whose hand I shake, ought to understand that, shouldn't you?"

If Azwaw replied something to this, I did not hear it. It is from the roof of his house, built by Far'oun the One-Eyed, that he saw the advent of Allah and Oqba, the event that burst upon his city in an uproar of endless neighing. In front of every house, a horse mounted by its rider had made a half turn and backed up several steps. Using their front hoofs like hatchets, they beat down against the wooden partitions, broke them open, backed up, and charged again.

It was on the only roof that did not collapse that day that Azwaw had a blinding cognition of what he had to do from then on. The battle of time was engaged. He was going to win it more rapidly than he had anticipated according to his plan. Without realizing it, the Emir had given him the idea of ideas, the arm of all arms. It was so simple after all.

5

Thirty years later, a flower is opening under my old man's eyes, slowly, with the joyous peace of a very small child that awakens. It is an oenothera, if my knowledge of words is accurate. As it opens, it is like a bird that gives the first note to the bird people as a greeting to the sun: hundreds of feet, all of the bed of oenotheras respond to him in unison in yellow-orange. I now know that it is the end of this God-given afternoon; I must arise and hasten to give the fourth call to prayer, the evening prayer.

I also know that in front of me and behind me there are other flower-beds, other flowers that have opened up in bloom or will blossom at a certain hour, the whole day long, or will not be long in closing up in a mauve of mauves, in the brilliant red of the hibiscus, the flame of the cannas, the multi-colored song of the calceolaria and of the phlox—an immense floral clock the whole length of the esplanade. Later on, from the top of the minaret, I will see them in all their splendor. I will give them my thanks. My true prayer will be for them, for my earth that engendered them, for the man that surrounded them with love. Yes, oh yes! Man can be his own god.

As I look at them in the setting sun, I shall also see, without attaching too much importance to it, the movement of ships leaving for new conquests and the flood tide of chariots and horses in the port area. Islam continues in space and in time. Sometimes someone says to me: "*Imam* Filani, explain to us the Book that you chant with your voice and with your soul. Why this and why that? What is the sense for God? And how is it that men have given it a totally different sense?" I look at the people who interrogate me, and I also look into the depths of myself, and, lo and behold, I do not find any words.

I am contented to be a simple Muslim in my conduct. That is quite enough for *them*. They point to me as an example. They venerate me. When I find myself up there, between sky and earth, I find my own again. It is toward them that I cry out the assembling, so that they will always stay on guard. Is Islam not a warning? I warn them with the only words I have at my disposal: ritual words. They understand me, that I know.

At the end of the esplanade and its enchantment is another delight: a *bellombra*, a gigantic tree with great white flowers in the form of cones. It is a garden in itself. And then there is the garden which is the ardently carved wood of arabesques of the tall door of the mosque that opens out before my path, a garden of the mosaic of all the shades of the sky and of the green grass, a musical garden, in these basins for ablutions, where the sound of water sings. *Our water.* The stairway that burrows into the minaret up to the platform turns in a spiral. I sit down on the first step. Is it I who weeps? I remember everything. My memory will survive me. I loved Oqba, as only I can love a man, a woman, or a land.

He died shortly after his arrival at the edge of the Atlantic. The sea was his supreme objective, which he owed to God. Once he had attained his goal, he turned back through the passes of the Atlas in pursuit of the rebel chief Kusaïla Lamzam and his partisans who thought they had been spared. It was his old tactic of the fox of the desert: to ignore the enemy encountered on route and then to turn brusquely and fall on him. I went with him. He had secured my services as the muezzin of the army. He had had some two thousand Aït Yafelmans incorporated among his troops, and he utilized them, against my wishes, to fight against their fellow Berbers. He had promised them and sworn to himself to make exemplary Muslims out of them. I betrayed my friend the Emir. I warned Kusaïla in the only way I could: from the top of the minaret, koranically. Oqba and his Bedouins perished in the gigantic ambush which had been set up for them. The only survivors were my Aït Yafelmans.

They never went back home to the mouth of Mother Spring. Never. The exodus began for them, at my orders, not in groups or even in families, but in individual dispersions throughout the countryside. Most of them arabized their names to pass unnoticed. They all sincerely converted to Islam, truly faithful among the faithful. As for me, from Aït Yafelman, I became Filani. the *imam* Filani. It was actually so simple, to become a part of the conquerors, body and soul.

Poor Oqba ibn Nafi! When I evoke your memory, it is above all your ardent faith that still fills me with fire. So very, very great in military art, and so small in time! Like all of those who preceeded you. Zouhaïr ibn Qaïs, Hassan ibn Nou'man, other generals walked in your footsteps and carried on your battles, spreading out through the space you cleared. Not one of them is worth the nail of your big toe. I followed them all. Through the glory of God that I sang from one city to another, they heard their own glory. It is for that reason, for that vanity, that they concede to me help and protection, give me their complete confidence, and honor me as an *imam* among *imam*s. From there where you are, you see as well as I do that Islam is breaking into pieces, that Islam that burned into you and burns into me, blotting out the voice of my past. I did not know the Prophet, despite my advanced age, neither him nor his companions of the first years. I did know you, Oqba. I loved you, but how can one love someone or something with the madness of forebears who at the same time you hate because you do not want a master? Never a master who makes a slave of you, even in the name of love? Who will win? The Berber or the Muslim? Me or me?

The steps are steep and high. I climb them one by one with difficulty. A very ancient patience, coming from the depths of the ages and bearing its fruit in the centuries to come, climbs with me. Who will be the first to the top? The believer or the pagan? The two of us will give the cry for prayer with the same faith. It must be so. It must be so by choice or by force, and for this world or the world beyond. Allah will judge and so will Mother Spring. But who is it then who weeps and suffers from one step to another as though it were a question of mounting a calvary? I don't know what to do anymore. Everything is engulfing me all at once. I no longer know who I am. Has time also shrunk me? If I listened to nothing but my past, I would do what I have been doing for the last thirty years.

At the very top of the minaret there is a platform with four angles. The call to prayer must resound turn by turn from these four angles, toward the four cardinal points, so that everyone will hear. I have used nothing but ceremonial formulas. For example:

"*Allah akbar!* I swear that there is no divinity but God. I swear that Mohammed is His prophet. Take care for prayer! Take care for your salvation!"

And nothing else. It is sufficient to first give the call in a previously determined direction to warn our brothers of a danger that threatens them. The time that I take, the tone of conviction that I use, clearly indicates to them, in a strong voice, the day and importance of the danger. That is how general Oqba ibn Nafi died, by reason of his very faith.

No, I am not a false witness. I was born here and I will die here. Our land will survive us all. Islam has flourished here as no flower ever has. But it had to create havoc to flourish; it killed a number of its sons, by the very hands that spoke in his name, in the name of God! Who knows if it will not waste away and die in its turn?

I think about time. That is why I stand guard and put on guard and at attention, five times a day, all of our people, and all of *theirs,* all of the descendants to come, Arabs or Berbers. With the last of my strength, I lift myself up the final step, and it is then that I hear someone call me by my name.

I recognize the executioner at once. There he is on the platform. He delicately runs his finger along the edge of a dagger. I am not afraid of him, even if everyone runs at the very sight of his shadow. No, not of him! He repeats my name:

"Azwaw Aït Yafelman."

Then he adds:

"I have finally found you!"

No, by Mother Spring and by God! It is not from this executioner of base works of Islam that my fear has come, but of the other man, over there on the other side of time. Still present, I suddenly see him. His name was Azoulay, a simple apparition. Seated in a grotto before a sword whose blade he caused to quiver, he had announced my destiny to me. I know that I still have some time to live, perhaps several years. I know also that from now on I will not be able to speak. Azoulay had said, "Not another word." My tongue will be cut off.

How am I to continue my mission? I have covered most of the earth in search of my daughter and my son. Who will take my place?

"When nothing else exists, the Sublime Face of God will subsist." That is what the Koran asserts, and it sings in my heart. People will pass by like a caravan all through time, and, at the end of time, there will still be the earth, the light, and the water of my country.

Lived at the mouth of the Oum-er-Bia.
The third decade of spring, year 681.
Written on an island in the Atlantic in 1982.

DRISS CHRAIBI was born in El Jadida, Morocco, in 1926. He was influenced in his early childhood by Islamic culture, but his later education in French schools opened him to Western values. He lived through the drama of his personal emancipation and the inner conflict of two civilizations, but although molded by both, Chraibi is sympathetic with neither. He soon became as critical of the entire Occidental world as he had been of the Islamic world.

Chraibi qualified as a chemical engineer, but turned entirely to writing in 1952, and in 1956 began work also in French radio and television, expressing throughout his work the conflict which has never ceased to inspire him because it is never resolved. Can man change the face of the earth to the point of fusing the civilizations of Orient and Occident?

HUGH HARTER, the translator of *Mother Spring*, received his B.A. in French and his Ph.D. in Spanish at Ohio State University, and his M.A., also in Spanish, at Mexico City College, now the University of the Americas. He is author or co-author of various books, reviews, and articles, and has translated from both the French and Spanish, including two other volumes of Chraibi published by Three Continents, *The Butts* and *Mother Comes of Age*, as well as the upcoming *The Simple Past*.

Dr. Harter was Director of the International Institute in Madrid from 1984 through 1987, and is at present working with overseas groups through Horizons for Learning, of which he is founder and president, and Cursos Americanos e Internaçionales in Segovia, Spain, of which he is founder and administrator.